Editor-in-Chief and Founder:
  Lyndon H. LaRouche, Jr.
Editorial Board: *Lyndon H. LaRouche, Jr. , Helga
  Zepp-LaRouche, Robert Ingraham, Tony
  Papert, Gerald Rose, Dennis Small, Jeffrey
  Steinberg, William Wertz*
Co-Editors: *Robert Ingraham, Tony Papert*
Managing Editor: *Nancy Spannaus*
Technology: *Marsha Freeman*
Books: *Katherine Notley*
Ebooks: *Richard Burden*
Graphics: *Alan Yue*
Photos: *Stuart Lewis*
Circulation Manager: *Stanley Ezrol*

INTELLIGENCE DIRECTORS
Counterintelligence: *Jeffrey Steinberg, Michele
  Steinberg*
Economics: *John Hoefle, Marcia Merry Baker,
  Paul Gallagher*
History: *Anton Chaitkin*
Ibero-America: *Dennis Small*
Russia and Eastern Europe: *Rachel Douglas*
United States: *Debra Freeman*

INTERNATIONAL BUREAUS
Bogotá: *Miriam Redondo*
Berlin: *Rainer Apel*
Copenhagen: *Tom Gillesberg*
Houston: *Harley Schlanger*
Lima: *Sara Madueño*
Melbourne: *Robert Barwick*
Mexico City: *Gerardo Castilleja Chávez*
New Delhi: *Ramtanu Maitra*
Paris: *Christine Bierre*
Stockholm: *Ulf Sandmark*
United Nations, N.Y.C.: *Leni Rubinstein*
Washington, D.C.: *William Jones*
Wiesbaden: *Göran Haglund*

ON THE WEB
e-mail: eirns@larouchepub.com
www.larouchepub.com
www.executiveintelligencereview.com
www.larouchepub.com/eiw
Webmaster: *John Sigerson*
Assistant Webmaster: *George Hollis*
Editor, Arabic-language edition: *Hussein Askary*

EIR (ISSN 0273-6314) *is published weekly
(50 issues), by EIR News Service, Inc.,
P.O. Box 17390, Washington, D.C. 20041-0390.
(703) 297-8434*

European Headquarters: E.I.R. GmbH, Postfach
Bahnstrasse 9a, D-65205, Wiesbaden, Germany
Tel: 49-611-73650
Homepage: http://www.eir.de
e-mail: info@eir.de
Director: Georg Neudecker

Montreal, Canada: 514-461-1557
eir@eircanada.ca

Denmark: EIR - Danmark, Sankt Knuds Vej 11,
basement left, DK-1903 Frederiksberg, Denmark.
Tel.: +45 35 43 60 40, Fax: +45 35 43 87 57. e-mail:
eirdk@hotmail.com.

Mexico City: EIR, Sor Juana Inés de la Cruz 242-2
Col. Agricultura C.P. 11360
Delegación M. Hidalgo, México D.F.
Tel. (5525) 5318-2301
eirmexico@gmail.com

Copyright: ©2017 EIR News Service. All rights
reserved. Reproduction in whole or in part without
permission strictly prohibited.

Canada Post Publication Sales Agreement
#40683579

Postmaster: Send all address changes to *EIR*, P.O.
Box 17390, Washington, D.C. 20041-0390.

Signed articles in *EIR* represent the views of the authors,
and not necessarily those of the Editorial Board.

Bob Mueller
Political Assassin

HELGA ZEPP-LAROUCHE

German Voters Reject Neoliberal Policy

Helga Zepp-LaRouche, who headed the slate of Germany's Civil Rights Movement Solidarity (BüSo) party, issued a short statement on Sept. 25, on the results of the nationwide elections of the previous day. A translation follows.

The political landslide that made the Alternative for Germany (AfD) the third largest party in Germany, as well as the winner in Saxony and the second largest force in the other states in the eastern part of the country, is yet another expression of the rejection of the neoliberal policy, which led to the Brexit and to the defeat of Hillary Clinton. Chancellor Angela Merkel's comment that her CDU/CSU is still the strongest group in the Bundestag against which no one could govern—just after some one million voters had walked away from it—shows that Mrs. Merkel is just as unwilling as Hillary Clinton to admit the reasons for her poor performance.

The parties in the Grand Coalition [CDU-SPD] were punished for their neo-liberal policy, for Hartz IV [a draconian labor market reform], and for the balanced budget policy, which have driven a growing percentage of the population into a precarious situation despite abundant tax revenues. What has occurred is exactly what I had already warned of in the Brexit, Trump's electoral victory and the referendum on changing the Italian constitution: This wave will continue until the injustices of the neoliberal policy have been eliminated.

The absurdity of this election campaign became clear in the so-called "elephants' round" [a talk show with the "heavyweight" candidates]. After the media and the candidates of the established parties had presented an election campaign void of any of the great issues, this talk-show, which took place after the election, turned into a slugfest, in which the participants at least gave free rein to their frustrations.

Anne Will [the television host] made a point of challenging Alexander Gauland [leader of the AfD] to admit that the AfD is only against things, but has no solutions. That is true, of course, but solutions are not to be found in the two major parties either, nor in the other three that are now in the Bundestag.

The elephant in the living room of the "elephants round" is the imminent new financial crash, which threatens to dwarf that of 2007-2008. The BüSo, together with friendly forces in different European nations and the United States, intends to increase its efforts for the implementation of a global Glass-Steagall system of bank separation as the only way to prevent uncontrolled chaos.

The BüSo will also escalate its campaign to get Germany and the other European countries to take up China's offer to work together in building the New Silk Road. That is the only way to develop the economies of Eastern and Central Europe and the Balkans, and to industrialize the Middle East and Africa. Building the New Silk Road offers the only avenue to surmounting the causes of the refugee wave in a humane way.

The BüSo fought for that during the election campaign, and will do so even more now. And our policy will prevail, despite the censorship, because it is in the interest of Germany and of all mankind.

Joint Development:
The Only Path to Peace in Korea

by Mike Billington

Sept. 24—It was true in the 1990s, as it was in 2002-2005, and is even more emphatically true today: Only a policy of engaging North Korea in a process of large scale regional infrastructure development can prevent the threat that war—perhaps global thermonuclear war—could break out on the Korean Peninsula.

When the Soviet Union fell in 1991, Lyndon and Helga LaRouche called for a New Silk Road, from Pusan to Rotterdam, as the necessary basis for ending the danger of global war, uniting East and West through the joint construction of multiple development corridors. The continuing isolation of North Korea was a key stumbling block to this vision of a new paradigm for global peace and development.

The United States and North Korea had never signed a peace treaty to end the Korean War in the 1950s, and confrontations occurred on a fairly regular basis. Constructing a rail corridor through the North, LaRouche posed, would not only complete the proposed New Silk Road, but would provide the North with a stake in this historic development process, and grounds for trust that it would not be attacked.

Today the world is being presented with an apparently unsurmountable conflict between North Korea and the United States, with the danger of war looming before us. The George W. Bush and Barack Obama administrations established an imperial policy demanding that all agreements and all talks would be suspended unless North Korea unilaterally ended all nuclear weapons programs and all missile development.

Now, President Donald Trump and North Korea's Kim Jong-un are trading barbs and insults, with both sides threatening military action.

Russian Foreign Minister Sergei Lavrov, speaking in New York on Sept. 22, called the exchange a "kindergarten fight between children" and urged calm. "We have to calm down the hot-heads and understand that we do need pauses, that we do need some contacts," Lavrov told a news conference at the United Nations on the sidelines of the annual General Assembly debate.

But Lavrov also referred to President Trump's speech at the UN as "remarkable," saying: "I think it's a very welcome statement, which we haven't heard from an American leader for a very long time." He referred to Trump's defense of the concept of national sovereignty, that "we do not seek to impose our way of life on anyone," and that, "I will always put America first, just as the leaders of your countries will always, and should always, put your countries first."

Helga Zepp-LaRouche pointed to the apparent contradiction between this and the threat in Trump's speech to destroy North Korea if it comes to war, calling it a "tale of two speeches."

But war is neither inevitable, nor even probable. The retired flag officers now serving in Trump's Cabinet have made clear that a war would be catastrophic for South Korea, the region, and the world. Trump has assured South Korean President Moon Jae-in that there will be no U.S. military action without South Korea's accord—and Moon has made clear that he will not allow a war, which would be particularly destructive of South Korea, whether or not nuclear weapons would have been deployed. Also, leading U.S. experts have argued that we can live with a nuclear-armed North Korea, as we have for 20 years already, because we have a powerful deterrent, and because Pyongyang is not suicidal. (See, for instance, Admiral Dennis Blair, former head of the U.S. Pacific Command and former Director of National Intelligence.)

But a solution is necessary, quickly. The 1995 Agreed Framework achieved by President Bill Clinton with Pyongyang—shutting down the North's production of weapons grade plutonium in exchange for a new, safer type of nuclear plant, and establishing IAEA inspectors in the country, while moving towards a peace agreement—was cancelled when George Bush and Dick Cheney came to power in 2001. Nonetheless, South Korean President Kim Dae-jung's Sunshine Policy toward the North proceeded, working closely with China and Russia, and with significant input from Lyndon LaRouche, leading to the opening of the Demilitarized Zone in 2002, and the reopening of the Iron Silk Road rail connections between the South and the North. (See http://www.larouchepub.com/eiw/public/2002/eirv29n37-20020927/eirv29n37-20020927_048-koreas_open_dmz_at_last_silk_roa.pdf.)

The UN Economic and Social Commission for Asia and Pacific (UNESCAP) issued a report in 2003 identifying the two rail routes from South Korea through North Korea, one to China and one to Russia, as part of the New Silk Road connections between Asia and Europe. Even Japan engaged in the process, as Prime Minister Kunichiro Koizumi travelled to Pyongyang and signed agreements with Kim Jung-il, the father of the current North Korean leader Kim Jong-un.

The Bush/Cheney neocons, however, were openly out to stop this process. Among other threats, Cheney and Deputy Secretary of State John Bolton threatened to begin boarding North Korean ships—i.e., piracy on the high seas—to stop alleged "proliferation of weapons of mass destruction."

China then took the initiative, with Russia, China, Japan, and South Korea, to invite the United States to join Six Party Talks to resolve the nuclear weapons issue peacefully. These began in 2003, leading to an agreement in 2005, again ending the North's weapons programs and bringing the IAEA inspectors back. Bush and Cheney managed to scuttle this peace and development agreement as well, claiming that a North Korean effort to place a satellite in space constituted a breach of the agreement against developing ICBMs—a clear case of "technological apartheid" under the guise of nonproliferation. Obama then adopted his provocative "strategic patience"—no talks until the North ended all nuclear development.

What should be obvious is that the Anglophile imperial forces in the United States, including Bush and Obama, *want* North Korea to have nuclear weapons. Their target is not North Korea, but China and Russia, maintaining the British imperial division of the world into East vs. West. As long as North Korea can be falsely claimed to be an imminent threat to the United States and its allies, there is an excuse to: encircle China with 60% of the U.S. naval nuclear armed forces (Obama's "Pivot to Asia"); place ABM systems and high-powered radar systems in a ring around China (THAAD); and deploy U.S. strategic forces in South Korea. These massive forces are obviously not needed to contain and deter North Korea. The target is China and Russia.

The solution is at hand. First, since President Trump is committed to cooperation with Russia and China, both in fighting terrorism and in economic development, he can be brought to work with them on a development orientation towards North Korea. The proposal by China and Russia for a double freeze—a pause on nuclear and missile tests in the North and a pause or scale-down of the United States-South Korean military exercises—is a sound basis for each side to show concern for the security of the other. Secretary of State Rex Tillerson has clearly stated that the United States will not impose regime change, or attack, or force reunification on North Korea, and despite Trump's extreme bargaining position approach, such restoration of talks is both possible and urgent.

President Putin, speaking with the press together with South Korean President Moon Jae-in at the Eastern Economic Forum in Vladivostok earlier this month, said:

> I would like to say that Russia is still willing to implement trilateral projects with the participation of North Korea. We could deliver Russian pipeline gas to Korea, and integrate the power lines and railway systems of Russia, the Republic of Korea, and North Korea. The implementation of these initiatives will be not only economically beneficial, but will also help build up trust and stability on the Korean Peninsula.

President Moon concurred, in keeping with his intent to revive the Sunshine Policy.

China is committed to this approach. Japan is now closely engaged with Russia in developing the Russian Far East, which depends on integrating North and South Korea into the process.

Trump can and must be convinced that to live up to his own challenge, stated in his UN speech, that, "We have it in our power, should we so choose, to lift millions of people from poverty, to help our citizens realize their dreams, and to ensure that new generations of children are raised free from violence, hatred and fear," that he should fully join with China and Russia in the New Silk Road process, including for a long-term, long overdue peace for the Korean people.

Open Letter
To President Donald Trump
In Defense of Columbus

by Liliana Gorini, Chairwoman, Movisol
Being circulated by the Schiller Institute, Sept. 20, 2017
http://www.schillerinstitute.org

President Donald Trump
The White House
Washington, D.C.

Mr. President:

As an Italian citizen and chairwoman of Movisol, Lyndon LaRouche's movement in Italy, I call on you to intervene in defense of Christopher Columbus and Columbus Day. The same people who are out to destroy the U.S. Presidency, led by Wall Street speculator George Soros (who destroyed the Italian lira in 1992), are also trying to eradicate history and culture not only in the United States, but internationally. Cardinal Nicholas of Cusa, his Italian collaborator Paolo del Pozzo Toscanelli, Columbus, Amerigo Vespucci, and others were part of a revolution in culture, art, geography, and science, which made the discovery of America possible. The deliberate explosion in human creativity that was the Italian Renaissance is a truly proud moment in all humanity's history, and not merely for Italians. The people who want to abolish Columbus Day, whether they are maliciously witting, or merely deluded, are out to also dismantle this Western cultural and scientific heritage.

It has always been the British, including the "cultural thought-police" associated with the British Museum, who have tried to downplay and dismantle the Italian Renaissance: to undermine its successful expedition to explore new lands, and to obfuscate and deny its mission to construct, "in a new world," a new and better sovereign nation-state, superior to those of Europe.

The United States of America eventually became that nation-state. This was a central, conscious part of the grand project of discovery, of Cusa, Toscanelli, and Christopher Columbus. There was nothing mistaken in that intention.

There is also nothing "sincerely mistaken" about this Dark Age movement to "bring down the statue." The Aug. 29 beheading of a statue of Columbus in the city of Yonkers, New York, reminds one of the beheading of 28 statues of religious figures in one day in October 1793, during the French Revolution—the same month that Marie Antoinette was guillotined. They called their movement "The Cult of Reason."

Similarly, it was the 1950s Con-

Creative Commons/
Statue of Christopher Columbus in Columbus, Ohio.

gress for Cultural Freedom (CCF) which actually tried to abolish culture and our historical roots from the 1950s on, and now apparently inspires gangs of protesters who, similar to ISIS in Palmyra and other jewels of culture in Syria, Iraq and Yemen, are out to destroy monuments and statues which remind the population of its inheritance. Beauty, in the classical, aesthetical sense, disturbs them.

Columbus and his trip of discovery was the result of the Italian Renaissance, which is, to this day, an important reference point for each Italian citizen in a moment of great crisis.

This is why there was an uproar here in Italy, and rightly so also in the Italian-American community in the United States, when we heard that a statue of Columbus was knocked down and that there are petitions to abolish Columbus Day and the Columbus Parade on Fifth Avenue.

What will be next? Tear down the city of Columbus in Ohio, which I visited years ago to admire its Columbus statue? Tear down the Brunelleschi Dome in Florence? Or the statue of Leonardo da Vinci in front of La Scala in Milan, which shows how Leonardo was not only a Renaissance genius, engineer, and painter, but also invented Bel Canto with his treatise, *De Vocie*, on the human voice?

We trust that you will intervene to defend this historical heritage, which cannot be forgotten, but should rather inspire a new Renaissance in culture, leading to scientific and economic cooperation between the United States and the rest of the world, including Russia and China. As Italians, we also call on you to keep your electoral promise and reinstate the Glass-Steagall Act, which would not only

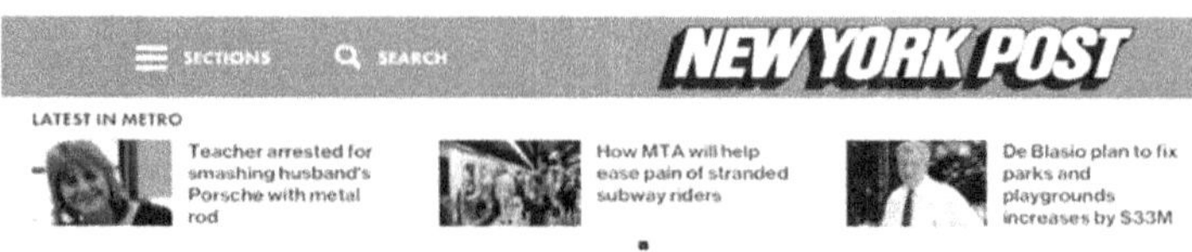

statue gets vandalized in NYC

Creative Commons/Daderot

Statue of Christopher Columbus by Gaetano Russo, Columbus Circle, New York City.

stop speculation and free up credit to build urgently needed infrastructure, but would also put an end to the excessive power of Wall Street, which is certainly behind, and financing, such misguided grass-roots campaigns. We are hoping to do the same here, and thus to jointly work with your Administration and other nations on new discoveries worthy of the true legacy of Christopher Columbus and Western civilization.

Liliana Gorini
Chairwoman of the Movimento Internazionale per i Diritti Civili Solidarietà (Movisol),
Milan, Italy

EIR Contents

www.larouchepub.com Volume 44, Number 39, September 29, 2017

Cover This Week

BOB MUELLER POLITICAL ASSASSIN

More Holes in Russia-Gate Narrative

New tests support the skepticism of U.S. intelligence veterans that Russia "hacked" the DNC's computers, pointing instead to a download of emails by an insider, write ex-NSA official William Binney and ex-CIA analyst Ray McGovern.

by William Binney and Ray McGovern

Sept. 20—It is no secret that our July 24 VIPS Memorandum for the President, entitled "Was the 'Russian Hack' an Inside Job?," gave rise to some questioning and controversy—nor was it a surprise that it was met with almost total silence in the mainstream media.

The ongoing U.S. media campaign against Russia has been so effective that otherwise intelligent people have been unable even to entertain the notion that they may have been totally misled by the intelligence community. The last time this happened, in 2003, after a year of such propaganda, the U.S. attacked Iraq [based] on fraudulent—not "mistaken"—intelligence.

Anticipating resistance from those allergic to rethinking "what everybody knows" about Russian "meddling," we based our VIPS analysis on forensic investigations that, oddly, the FBI had bent over backwards to avoid. In other words, we relied on the principles of physics and the known capability of the Internet in early July 2016.

We stand by our main conclusion that the data from the intrusion of July 5, 2016, into the Democratic National Committee's computers, an intrusion blamed on "Russian hacking," was not a hack but rather a download/copy onto an external storage device by someone with physical access to the DNC.

That principal finding relied heavily on the speed with which the copy took place—a speed much faster than a hack over the Internet could have achieved at the time—or, it seems clear, even now. Challenged on that conclusion—often by those conducting experiments within the confines of a laboratory—we have conducted and documented additional tests to determine the speeds that can be achieved now, more than a year later.

To remind: We noted in the VIPS memo that on July 5, 2016, a computer directly connected to the DNC server or DNC Local Area Network, copied 1,976 megabytes of data in 87 seconds onto an external storage device. That yields a transfer rate of **22.7 megabytes per second (MBps)**.

Recent Tests

Over the last few weeks, we ran three tests to determine how quickly data could be exfiltrated from the U.S. across the Atlantic to Europe.

• First, we used a 100 megabits-per-second (mbps) line to pull data from a one-gigabyte file to Amsterdam. The peak transfer speed was **.8 MBps**.

• Second, we used a commercial DSL (Digital Subscriber Line) to send the same one-gigabyte file to a commercial DSL in Amsterdam. The peak transfer speed was **1.8 MBps**.

• Third, we pushed the same one-gigabyte file from a data center in New Jersey to a data center in the UK. The peak transfer speed was **12 MBps**.

None of these attempts achieved anything close to the average rate of **22.7 megabytes per second** evident in the July 5, 2016 download/copy associated with the DNC. In fact, this happens to be the speed

typical of a transfer to a USB-2 external storage device. We do not think this pure coincidence; rather, it is additional evidence of a local download.

We are preparing further trans-Atlantic testing over the next few weeks.

Some researchers have noted that some partitioning of the data might have occurred in the U.S., allowing for a transfer to be made at the measured speed over the Internet, and that this could have made possible a hack from the other side of the Atlantic. One of our associate investigators has found a way to achieve this kind of data partitioning and later transfer.

In theory, this would be one possible way to achieve such a large-data transfer, but we have no evidence that anything like this actually occurred. More important, in such a scenario, the National Security Agency would have chapter and verse on it, because such a hack would have to include software to execute the partitioning and subsequent data transfer. NSA gives the highest priority to collection on "execution software."

Must Americans, apparently including President Donald Trump, remain in a Russia-did-it-or-could-have-maybe-might-have-done-it subjunctive mood on this important issue—one that has been used to inject Cold War ice into relations with Russia? The answer is absolutely not. Rather, definitive answers are at hand.

How can we be so confident? Because NSA alumni now active in Veteran Intelligence Professionals for Sanity (VIPS) are intimately familiar with NSA's capabilities and practice with respect to bulk capture and storage of fiber-optic communications. Two of us actually devised the systems still in use, and Edward Snowden's revelations filled in remaining gaps. Today's NSA is in position to clear up any and all questions about intrusions into the DNC.

In sum, we are certain that the truth of what actually happened—or didn't happen—can be found in the databases of NSA. We tried to explain this to President Barack Obama in a VIPS Memorandum of Jan. 17, just three days before he left office, noting that NSA's known programs are fully capable of capturing—and together with liaison intelligence services do capture—all electronic transfers of data.

Our Jan. 17 Memorandum included this admonition: "We strongly suggest that you ask NSA for any evidence it may have indicating that the results of Russian hacking were given to WikiLeaks." … "If NSA cannot give you that information—and quickly—this would probably mean it does not have any."

We also appealed to Obama in his final days in office

to order the chiefs of the NSA, FBI and CIA to the White House and have them lay all their cards on the table about "Russian hacking," and show him what tangible evidence they might have—not simply their "assessments." We added, "We assume you would not wish to hobble your successor with charges that cannot withstand close scrutiny." Having said this, we already were reaching the assumption that there was no real evidence to back the "assessments" up.

FBI: Not Leaning Forward

The FBI could still redeem itself by doing what it should have done as soon as the DNC claimed to have been "hacked." For reasons best known to former FBI Director James Comey, the Bureau failed to get whatever warrant was needed to confiscate the DNC servers and computers to properly examine them.

In testimony to the House Intelligence Committee six months ago, Comey conceded "best practice is always to get access to the machines themselves." And yet he chose not to. And his decision came amid frenzied charges by senior U.S. officials that Russia had committed "an act of war."

But is it not already too late for such an investigation? We hope that, at this point, it is crystal clear that the answer is: No, it is not too late. All the data the FBI needs to do a proper job is in **NSA databases**—including data going across the Internet to the DNC server and then included in their network logs.

If President Trump wants to know the truth, he can order the FBI to do its job and NSA to cooperate. Whether the two and the CIA would obey such orders is an open question, given how heavily invested all three agencies are in their evidence-impoverished narrative about "Russian hacking."

Let us close with the obvious. All three agencies have been aware all along that NSA has the data. One wonders why it should require a Presidential order for them to delve into that data and come up with conclusions based on fact, as opposed to "assessing."

This article also appeared in consortiumnews.com, *Sept. 20.*

William Binney (williambinney0802@comcast.net) worked for NSA for 36 years, retiring in 2001 as the technical director of world military and geopolitical analysis and reporting; he created many of the collection systems still used by NSA. Ray McGovern (raymcgovern.com) was a CIA analyst for 27 years; from 1981 to 1985 he briefed the President's Daily Brief one-on-one to President Reagan's most senior national security officials.

Exposing the 'Russia-Gate' Lie

On September 26, a UK citizen, writing under the pseudonym "Adam Carter," responded by email to several short questions from Executive Intelligence Review *regarding his role in uncovering numerous inconsistencies in the reporting on Russia-gate—most prominently with respect to the purported Russian hacker "Guccifer 2.0."*

EIR: You are very active on the Russia-Gate/Guccifer 2.0 issue. Recently, on Sept 17, you wrote about reaching out to the foreign embassies in London as "Phase 5" of your actions. Could you tell our readers how you've been weighing in on the Russia-gate discussion, and other ways you've been acting to shape the debate and avoid a needless nuclear war with Russia?

Adam Carter: As you may know, I've been researching the topic of Guccifer 2.0 since the beginning of the year (after considering various anomalies and deciding to independently investigate). While quite a lot of new information has come about from this (with a lot of help from co-contributors and other analysis from independent researchers/analysts), the mainstream press have been unwilling to report on the discoveries.

Knowing that we're up against systems that have much to lose from the collapse of the erroneous mainstream narrative on Guccifer 2.0's origins (including budgets and contracts worth billions over time, reputations of politicians, reputations of many in the press, reputations of cyber security experts and firms, etc.), I've always known it was going to be an uphill battle that would take a long time.

So, when one of the more recent additions (from an analyst working under the pseudonym "Forensicator") caught the eye of several VIPS [Veteran Intelligence Professionals for Sanity] members and we subsequently had Forensicator's work and some of the research from my site cited by them, I wanted to make sure we made optimal use of the opportunity to increase exposure of the research and evidence.

We were fortunate that [former IBM IT executive] Skip Folden reached out to us on behalf of VIPS, and since then, both Forensicator and I have tried to answer any of their questions and let them know of any of our new discoveries, test results, etc.

As you know, an article in *The Nation*, "A New Report Raises Big Questions About Last Year's DNC Hack," caused quite a stir recently too. It did make

some conclusions that weren't necessarily stated in the original research it drew upon (likely from inference due to the archive contents and other information relevant to the date, but not necessarily declared anywhere as a hack on that date), and it appears that a metaphorical third party statement, I believe, was reported as though it was a literal one.

In addition to researching and reporting on numerous discoveries made, I've always tried to consider strategy with regard to getting the information out. Throughout the past nine months, I've consistently considered such issues as dealing with media blackouts, propaganda, the use of logical fallacies to degrade and disrupt the information, and other factors. As part of that, I also planned several phases for my own efforts, with the latter phases being direct contact with politicians and, pending legal advice, possibly with DNC donors whose details were published (though I'm likely to leave that to a legal firm if I find one that wishes to pursue it).

When I saw other writers attack the article in *The Nation* (and in most cases through a straw-man attack on the calculated transfer speeds and conclusions drawn from them), including presenting themselves as debunking the underlying research, I knew I had to make sure that as many of the articles that were unfair or deceptive were challenged, and that those seeking to mislead their readers were skewered for every effort to manipulate.

While all that was going on (and as continues to crop up from time to time!), I noticed in a follow-up article that Skip Folden had mentioned sending a more detailed report ["Non-Existent Foundation for Russian Hacking Charge"] to the Office of the Special Counsel and Deputy Attorney General. Seeing his direct action reminded me of the fact that there was still a phase of the efforts I'd previously planned out that remained— phase #5: contact every foreign embassy in London (as I'm from the UK) and advise representatives of as many nations as possible about the likelihood of false attribution of Guccifer 2.0 to Russia, and how it was being exploited by politicians and mainstream media to manufacture consent for war.

Knowing that Skip's report may remain unacknowledged and possibly ignored by the recipients, it seemed it would be a good time to draw attention from around the world on the investigations being carried out. I wanted to try to make sure there was increased scrutiny on the recipients of the report, and how they are reacting to being provided notification of exculpatory evidence and of problems with the JAR [Joint Analysis Report] and ICA [Intelligence Community Assessment] reports (and so far, it looks like they've failed to acknowledge it).

So I wrote to every embassy that I could in London, to try to bring more attention to the issue, and to try to put some pressure on those that should be investigating thoroughly and in good faith.

EIR: What advice would you offer activists, on this issue, and more generally?

Carter: Failing to succeed is far better than failing to have tried at all.

If direct action is correspondence, try to draw public attention to the fact that recipients have been informed, and then put their inaction and disregard on a pedestal. Politicians and "deep state" institutions will try to ignore things that are inconvenient for them until doing so becomes damaging to their own reputations, and sometimes you have to provoke a situation where you can demonstrate that someone is acting shamefully or betraying public trust.

Regarding online/social-media activism—there is an information war on: there are reputation management firms that are paid a lot to degrade information, to cause confusion and conflation, and to dispute claims through the use of logical fallacies. As such, it's good to be aware of their tactics, able to identify them quickly and call them out. I'd recommend the following links for some interesting and helpful information on the topic:

- Thou Shalt Not Commit Logical Fallacies
- Carlo Kopp, Considerations on Deception Techniques Used in Political and Product Marketing
- Carlo Kopp, Classical Deception Techniques and Perception Management vs. the Four Strategies of Information Warfare
- Institute for Propaganda Analysis, How To Detect Propaganda
- Glenn Greenwald, How Covert Agents Infiltrate the Internet to Manipulate, Deceive, and Destroy Reputations.

If engaging in direct action, try to always do things in a group, the bigger the better—it helps with confidence and makes it more difficult for activists to be singled out and unfairly treated.

Personal Background

EIR: Tell us about yourself, in terms of your motivations and decisions to put so much effort into this matter. How do you see your role in history?

Carter: I'm a citizen of the UK with interests in technology, digital arts, global politics, science, media and more. I've been in awe of America since I was a kid, and over the last 15 years (due to 9/11 and the response from both our governments to it), and have become fascinated by U.S. politics (and the foreign policy objectives our nations seem to share in many areas).

For the past 15 years, I've worked in website and web application development. While this is my primary area of expertise, I have a much broader interest in technology, and try to stay up to date with new developments whether in development, 3D design, or less creative (but still essential) fields such as information security. Inherently in what I do, I'm defending clients from hackers, malware, botnets, etc., and have written software that scans for malware from any website root it's installed on.

Going further back, in my teens, I disassembled and cracked software and more (back in the 16-bit era). I was no stranger to BBSs [bulletin board systems] and did have a brief phase of being a black-hat hacker. However, that was all a long time ago. I'm now a director of a business with two kids and a mortgage, and the closest I now come to mischief is having the audacity to call out what I strongly feel is—at least as far as it pertains to Guccifer 2.0—a false narrative built upon deceit.

So, essentially, you could say I'm an ex-hacker calling out a fake hacker.

Motivation To Investigate

Around December of 2016, I noticed Guccifer 2.0 was being cited a lot in the media alongside "Russian hacking is an act of war!" rhetoric, and some specious claims about Putin ordering the hacking and/or directing the use of hacked materials. I noticed it become a highly polarizing issue, and it got me thinking back to the many inconsistencies in the alleged hacker's actions and words, the blatant nonsense of the supposed "Clinton Foundation Hack"; also how weird it was that Guccifer 2.0 was supposedly a skilled hacker, yet, lacking the egotistic flair skilled hackers are renowned for, adopted the name of someone else and stuck "2.0"

on the end. I then thought about the headlines Guccifer 2.0 had generated and how so much of the material he released was of little to no impact to the Clinton campaign or the DNC's leadership. It didn't make sense and yet this "hacker" was being used as part of the justification. To me, something just didn't seem right with it.

Towards the end of December, with time off work, my curiosity grew. I started searching, going back to old articles, trying to make more sense of what Guccifer 2.0 was. It was no good—everything was spread out and the facts I had gathered lacked chronological context. So, to get a better understanding of what Guccifer 2.0 was, I decided to construct a timeline with everything I could find in terms of primary and secondary sources relating to Guccifer 2.0, with dates, key revelations, and including the links to the source articles and links to archived copies of the pages.

I read all the articles while gathering them (and eliminated tertiary sources that added nothing to the sources they were citing). I then read through everything in sequence again at the end.

Initial Discoveries

It didn't take long before I found an enormous number of anomalies and inconsistencies where there shouldn't be any, as well as some odd correlations where none should exist. It was baffling, but one thing I was sure of was that this was not a genuine hacker, nor was it someone who truly intended to hurt the DNC leadership or the Clinton campaign. (ThreatConnect discredited his breach claims; he never mentioned any of the significantly more damaging revelations exposed in the emails released by Wikileaks; and his leaks were mostly junk—and mysteriously, this supposedly skilled hacker could only produce material from the Democratic Party.)

Knowing that hackers are more prone to security lapses at the beginning of an operation and at points of excitement (I was able to predict the moment when Sabu of Lulzsec had been compromised by the FBI, on the basis of something I've only ever seen occur with Compromised-Sabu and Guccifer 2.0), I decided to review the first batch of files and activities of Guccifer 2.0 on the day he emerged.

I then spotted Warren Flood's name, not just on one document but on three different documents, and something else—the document creation dates were all June

15 (the same day as this "hacker" emerged), and the three with Flood's name on them had identical creation times. (To be clear, Flood is very likely innocent, and his name is likely to be an indicator of which computer was used to produce the initial pre-tainted template document.)

I thought it was odd, because those that had reported on it seemed to have made no mention of it. In fact, an article published at Gawker actually misreported the date of the first document's metadata.

Learning What Guccifer 2.0 Was

I started to see how Guccifer 2.0's behavior did more to undermine and distract from WikiLeaks than anything else, and soon realized the significance of what I was looking at.

I then had an interaction with a user on Reddit, u/tvor_22, and, when looking at the initial documents Guccifer 2.0 released, he made a discovery that helped clarify what we were looking at. Essentially, the documents were constructed in a deliberate manner to have Russian language metadata and stylesheets in them.

Knowing this was an attempt to blame Russians for leaks, and seeing that it was now being exploited by some who were coupling it up with hawkish rhetoric, I knew it needed opposing, but also knew more investigation was needed, as a strong multi-faceted argument would be required to go up against a well-established mainstream narrative—and one that had just been bolstered by various statements made by intelligence agencies, and was aggressively promoted by many in the mainstream press.

I considered the facts:
• I knew Guccifer 2.0 was a lie of some sort. • I'm outside of the U.S. (so, was hopefully at less risk of interception or worse). • I've successfully attributed a hack to perpetrators before. • I'm probably less emotionally invested in the election outcome than most Americans, which may help carry out an impartial investigation. • I already knew much that had been unreported or misreported. • I was prepared to investigate in good faith, turning over every stone eventually and being transparent about discoveries made. • I thought, as I'd already come this far and figured out things that had been missed, maybe trying to carry out a more extensive investigation and take things further wasn't necessarily beyond my capabilities.

I didn't welcome the risk, but the guilt I'd feel from allowing an unnecessary conflict to occur would be completely unbearable, especially when I knew I was in a better position to speak out about it than most.

While that, of course, means the path I've been walking the last nine months hasn't been an easy one, there have been some very positive things too, and it's these that give me the stamina and determination to keep pushing forward.

I've been extremely fortunate to have gained some valuable support and contributions from a number of talented and thoughtful people (sometimes directly through my site, sometimes separately through analysis they release on their own sites). Merging paths with some key members of VIPS as well as with a highly proactive contributor to their efforts has also been a very welcome blessing too.

Regarding your question, "How do you see your role in history?"—I don't want my ego or personality to get in the way, especially not at such a critical time. Maybe one day I'll be able to contemplate that, but for now, I'm just someone who tried to do the right thing when he realized everybody had been lied to.

For now though, there's still much to do and still many that are yet to wake up.

Robert Mueller Is an Amoral Legal Assassin: He Will Do His Job If You Let Him

by Barbara Boyd

Sept. 23—Robert Swan Mueller III—the special prosecutor tasked to take down the President of the United States—is, as his name suggests, a product of elite private schools and universities. He is uniformly and soberly praised in the national news media as incorruptible, fair-minded "honest Bob," "straitlaced Bobby three sticks." This image, we shall show, is a brazenly false, Washington, D.C. public relations pitch, created for the credulous.

In reality, Robert Swan Mueller III is about as corrupt as they come, if necessary bending and twisting the law every which way to serve the goals of those who provide him assignments. The might of the prosecutorial function and the institutions he serves dictate what is right for him, rather than the unbiased pursuit of justice the law envisions for his vocation.

In what he says was a defining moment, Mueller broke ranks, after college, to serve in the Vietnam War as a Marine. After that he never wanted to do anything but prosecute. His appointment as special prosecutor caps a long career in which he has envisioned himself to be a stern and willing warrior, a dutiful Marine, acting on behalf of whatever evil scheme his superiors present to him, and using whatever means seems necessary to execute it.

In recent weeks, organizers for the LaRouche movement have been repeatedly told by citizens they meet:

Robert Swan Mueller III

"It looks like President Trump is getting the 'LaRouche treatment.'" The two men could not be more different in station, or cultural and intellectual achievement. LaRouche is a world-historical genius in the mold of Gottfried Leibniz. But, both men touched what has amounted to the third rail of American politics since Franklin Roosevelt's death. They threatened the post-War Anglo-American British imperial system. LaRouche did so directly, continuously, and explicitly by name. Trump has done so implicitly, by rejecting perpetual war, seeking better relations with Russia, calling for imposition of Glass-Steagall banking separation, endorsing what he refers to as the American System of political economy, and promising massive infrastructure development and a modern manufacturing platform for productive jobs.

In both cases, as we shall see, the British explicitly demanded scalps, based on a perceived threat to them, most specifically located in the desire for a collaborative relationship with Russia and an end to the "unipolar" framework of relationships between nations. In both cases, a controlled media unleashed an incessant barrage of ugly, salacious, and defamatory coverage, day-in day-out, to create the popular conditions for a criminal prosecution. While there were and are many other players in these Kabuki dances—compromised and terrorized politicians and judges, and an intelligence community which functions as the gendarme of our Orwellian police state—the blunt instrument chosen for the hit was Robert Mueller. Along the way, between the two assignments, Robert Mueller played a hugely significant role in covering up the Saudi/British role in the murders of almost 3,000 Americans on September 11, 2001, and the wholesale destruction of the United States Constitution which followed in its wake—a role which, if thoroughly examined, constitutes obstruction of justice, among other crimes.

This dossier will walk you through Mueller's career based on what is readily and publicly available. It is a trail of prosecutorial misconduct, including what former Senator Bob Graham calls "aggressive deception" of the U.S. Congress and the public concerning the events of September 11, 2001, and includes a major role in the creation of the post-9/11 surveillance state which has eviscerated and destroyed the Fourth Amendment and the rest of our Constitution's Bill of Rights. Those who work inside our modern Leviathan can surely point to other malfeasance, and we invite you to pile on—please, expose it. You owe no less to your oath to the Constitution of the United States.

The LaRouche Case—An Attempted Murder and then a Legal One

On Aug. 27, 1982, a Top Secret letter was sent from the British government to the FBI. That letter itself remains classified to this day, but it is clear from the FBI's response to it, from its unclassified attachments, and from subsequent actions, what the British were demanding. On Sept. 24, 1982, under the subject-heading "Re: Lyndon LaRouche and the Executive Intelligence Review," FBI counterintelligence chief James Nolan responded to the British demands as follows:

> We would like to reiterate our conclusion that, while many of the harassment activities of the NCLC and the themes promoted by NCLC publications, such as *EIR*, are often propitious to Soviet disinformation and propaganda interests, there is no direct evidence that the Soviets are directing or funding LaRouche or his organization. It is entirely plausible, however, that the Soviets have developed or may be developing sources within the NCLC who are in a position to interject Soviet-inspired views into NCLC activities and publications. It is likely that the Soviets will attempt to capitalize on or exploit NCLC sentiments that are parallel to or promote Soviet foreign policy objectives. At the same time, the Soviets will probably have to balance the advantages of exploiting the NCLC with the dangers of being associated with a bizarre and often unpredictable organization. For your information, under the domestic security guidelines set forth by the Attorney General, the FBI does not have an active investigation of Lyndon LaRouche or the NCLC.

As we shall see, this is the same British smear, in the same British speculative language, used to paint Donald Trump with the "Russian dupe" brush. That allegation, of LaRouche activity on behalf of a foreign power, the Russians, unleashed a full spectrum of intelligence agency weapons, free from Constitutional constraints under the Reagan Administration's Executive Order 12333 and subsequent renditions governing classified counterintelligence activities, particularly the subsequent versions of E.O. 12333 put into place after September 11, 2001.

We document below some of what LaRouche was doing to provoke the British call for his head in 1982. His activities included back-channel negotiations with the Russians concerning the Strategic Defense Initiative on behalf of the CIA and National Security Council. He met with Indian Prime Minister Indira Gandhi and Mexico's President José López Portillo, seeking a completely new monetary system, not controlled by the City of London, Wall Street and allied institutions, which would finance high technology development, completely transforming North-South relations. President López Portillo implemented LaRouche's proposals during the Mexican debt crisis in 1982, sending the Anglo-Americans into rug-chewing fits.

This British demand to the FBI immediately followed a letter, on Aug. 19, 1982, from Henry Kissinger to FBI Director William Webster, demanding that LaRouche be investigated for "harassing" Kissinger. This is the same Henry Kissinger who, in a speech at the Royal Institute of International Affairs on May 10, 1982, had openly declared himself to be a British agent of influence. While endorsing Churchill's "rigid" anti-Soviet policies and British colonialism over "naïve" American idealists, Kissinger remarked on his service to the British while in the U.S. government:

> The British were so matter of factly helpful that

C-SPAN

David Abshire

EIRNS/Stuart Lewis

Leo Cherne

Library of Congress

Edward Bennett Williams

they became a participant in internal American deliberations, to a degree never before practiced between sovereign nations. In my period in office, the British played a seminal role in certain American bilateral negotiations with the Soviet Union. Indeed, they helped draft the key document. In my White House incarnation then [as National Security Adviser] I kept the British Foreign Office better informed and more closely engaged than I did the American State Department.

William Casey

Cherne, and Edward Bennett Williams, demanded that an FBI investigation, under Executive Order 12333, be opened on LaRouche, based on "harassment" of Henry Kissinger and possible foreign funding, *under the guidelines or otherwise.* The British demand was going to be implemented.

In April 1983 and thereafter, New York investment banker John Train convened a series of salons attended by nominally private organizations, prominent journalists living off intelligence community leaks, and government intelligence operatives, to plan and implement a defamatory campaign against Lyndon LaRouche. The avowed aim of the meetings was to create the popular conditions for criminal prosecution.

What Kissinger called "harassment" by LaRouche, was widespread exposure of the British-agent aspect of his *curriculum vitae,* among other issues. These include Kissinger's 1974 "NSSM 200" document calling for drastic population reduction in the Third World by any means necessary in order to conserve raw materials for colonialist looting, threats to Italy's Prime Minister Aldo Moro shortly before his kidnapping and murder, contentions of similar action by the Bhutto family of Pakistan concerning the murder of former President Zulfikar Ali Bhutto, and numerous documented war crimes.[1]

On Jan. 12, 1983, the President's Foreign Intelligence Advisory Board, comprising David Abshire, Leo

In 1982, the Anglophilic CIA Director, William Casey, had tasked CIA psychological warfare and propaganda expert Walter Raymond to oversee a program of psychological warfare and "perception management" by the Reagan Administration, a program largely overseen by Vice President George H.W. Bush. Under provisions of the new executive order governing intelligence and counterintelligence operations, EO 12333, psy-ops and propaganda operations, formerly conducted on foreign targets by the CIA, were to be farmed out to private entities under such rubrics as Project Democracy, the National Endowment for Democracy, Freedom House, the League for Industrial Democracy,

---

1. Dr. Kissinger has recently appeared to play a useful role in arguing against war with Russia and China, against the mad Neo-Conservatives.

and similarly designated entities. psy-ops and "perception management" were also to be targetted domestically in counterintelligence operations. To start such counterintelligence operations, a credible allegation had to be presented that a domestic target was operating on behalf of a foreign power, such as the Russians.

John Train's investment company partner, Thomas J. Devine, a former CIA employee, had partnered with George H.W. Bush in the Zapata Oil company, during Bush's time as an oil man in Texas. Many believe that Zapata was a CIA proprietary. Train himself was the former editor of the Congress for Cultural Freedom's *Paris Review,* and was engaged, at the time of his LaRouche salons, in running black propaganda operations for the CIA against the Russians during the war in Afghanistan. Train's work in Afghanistan was coordinated with Walter Raymond.

Court testimony in the LaRouche cases and follow-up investigations revealed that the Train salons were attended by Roy Godson, a long-time British intelligence-connected operative deployed under the CIA's Jay Lovestone and James Jesus Angleton, and, at that time, a consultant to PFIAB and the National Security Council; by John Rees, an FBI functionary; Mira Lansky Boland of the Anti-Defamation League of B'nai B'rith (ADL); representatives of Freedom House, long a CIA proprietary associated with PFIAB's Leo Cherne; financier Richard Mellon Scaife; Pat Lynch of NBC; reporters for *Reader's Digest, Business Week,* the *Wall Street Journal,* and the *New Republic*; "investigative reporter" Dennis King who was employed by the League for Industrial Democracy; Chip Berlet; neo-conservative colleagues of Train; and others described by participants as "gentlemen with government connections." The representative from Freedom House provided the briefings on LaRouche to those assembled.

Train's salons resulted in a barrage of articles portraying LaRouche as violent, a racist, megalomaniacal, and an authoritarian anti-Semitic extremist—calculated and horrific, poisonous lies designed to nullify any positive response to LaRouche's actual ideas.

John Train

These ID-format lies are deliberately designed to create "cognitive dissonance," as it is known in the psy-ops trade. President Trump has been consistently portrayed with similar psy-ops ID-format defamations.

Defamatory broadcasts and articles by the Train meeting participants were concocted, and entirely fake versions of LaRouche's ideas and work were spewed to the public. *NBC News,* for example, presented a completely fake picture of *EIR's* groundbreaking exposé of the drug trade, *Dope Inc.,* which had become a bible for DEA agents in the War on Drugs. *Dope Inc.* proved that the British were actively promoting drug legalization for population pacification purposes, as they had done historically in the opium wars against China, and that British financial institutions, including banks and funds directly associated with the Royals, were dependent upon and subsisting on drug money-laundering proceeds. The book's contentions have been ratified repeatedly over the years in such cases as that of the HongKong and Shanghai Banking Corporation (HSBC). NBC repeatedly broadcast, however, that LaRouche's War on Drugs consisted of the claim that the Queen herself was out on the street corner peddling dime bags of heroin.

Even more astoundingly, NBC's Patricia Lynch claimed, in a prominent NBC news feature, that LaRouche had ordered the assassination of President Jimmy Carter by remote controlled bomb. She admitted that she relied for this preposterous claim on a notorious FBI informant and other "non-public" information provided to her by former CIA counterintelligence chief James J. Angleton, other CIA sources, and sources in the FBI. In March 1986, a collaboration between Irwin Suall from the ADL and the East German Stasi, produced the sensational and completely fabricated claim that LaRouche had played a role in the assassination of Swedish Prime Minister Olaf Palme. Richard Mellon Scaife and the CIA's Smith Richardson Foundation funded a book-length defamatory dossier by Dennis King as a result of the Train meetings, which became the central resource for a relentless anti-LaRouche hate campaign.

Do such wild, salacious assertions remind you, in any way, of the deliberately gross and fake dossier on President Trump, prepared by the highest levels of British intelligence for circulation to the American public? You know—the so-called "Pee Dossier" by MI6 agent Christopher Steele, that claims that the President cavorted with Russian prostitutes on a bed slept in by the Obamas?

What Did LaRouche Do?

The attachments to the British demand letter to the FBI include a published statement by LaRouche demanding that the Monroe Doctrine be enforced in support of Argentina with respect to the British-instigated Malvinas War. In the document, LaRouche contrasts British imperial looting policies with the "American System" as defined by Lincoln's economist Henry C. Carey. Addressing those in Congress siding with Britain against Argentina during the Malvinas crisis, LaRouche said:

> How shaken are these representatives at Britain's plight, the same representatives who have sat by and let U.S. industrial power be destroyed by British system economics, watched millions of Third World children starve for lack of technology exports, and raved about the fascist oppressions of the only energy source, nuclear power, that could turn the situation around! ... The imposition of the Monroe Doctrine and reassertion of the commitment to republican sovereignty can put the United States back on the road to fulfilling our national mission. Kicking the British Tories out of the Senate should be followed within minutes with kicking Tory Volcker out of the Fed, and restarting American industry once again.

The second attachment to the British demand letter is a leaflet announcing an *EIR* forum focused on developing the economies of the Middle East, and exposing the role of British intelligence in creating and funding Muslim Brotherhood Islamic fundamentalism. The second topic for the *EIR* forum concerned an exposé of the role of the British Secret Services in the then ongoing Soviet succession struggle. Other attachments to the British demand letter to the FBI remain classified.

A review of LaRouche's activities in 1982, the year the British called for his head, reveals that LaRouche's

Mexico's President José López Portillo addresses the UN General Assembly.

policies were gaining ground on every front and that he had developed a substantial following in U.S. intelligence and military circles in support of those policies, including in President Reagan's National Security Council. He also posed a direct challenge to British control of the world's economy, through the City of London, Wall Street, and aligned government institutions, and the hegemonic British economic nostrums of free trade and speculative capitalism.

From December 1981 through February 1983, LaRouche had been tasked first by the CIA and then by President Reagan's National Security Council to conduct back-channel discussions with Soviet representatives on what became President Reagan's Strategic Defense Initiative. Beginning as early as 1978, LaRouche had been calling for U.S.-Soviet collaboration in developing beam-weapon defenses to incoming thermonuclear missiles, replacing the insane Anglo-American doctrine of Mutually Assured Destruction with one of Mutually Assured Survival. At the same time as he met secretly with Soviet representatives, LaRouche and his associates campaigned publicly for the concept. President Reagan announced adoption of the SDI in a surprise televised address on March 23, 1983.

In April 1982, Lyndon and Helga LaRouche traveled to India where they met with Prime Minister Indira Gandhi, along with scientists, parliamentarians, industrialists, and economists. In his presentations, LaRouche stressed that the developing sector must band together, creating credit for large scale infrastructure development along lines consistent with Hamilton's system of political economy. In this endeavor, the British system of Malthusian zero population growth, primitive "sustainable development," and debt slavery—the policies of the World Bank and the IMF—would be condemned as genocidal and abandoned. True human progress could be scientifically and reliably measured, LaRouche said, by the metric he had discovered, potential relative population density, ensuring continuous progressive economic development.

In May 1982, LaRouche met with Mexican President José López Portillo, and immediately followed that meeting with a document entitled "Operation Juarez," a battle plan for reorganizing the already bankrupt world financial system based on physical-economic development. LaRouche proposed that the nations of Ibero-America use their collective strategic leverage as debtor nations to unite in a common economic bloc and unilaterally declare a restructuring of their debts and the establishment of a new, just monetary order. The formation of an International Development Bank among these nations would serve as a coordinating agency for planning investments and trade expansion among the member republics. "If a sufficient portion of the Ibero-American nations enter into such an agreement, the result is the assembly of one of the most powerful economies in the world from an array of individually weak powers . . . the Ibero-American continent would rapidly emerge as a leading economic power of the world, an economic super-power."

In August, López Portillo tried to bring Argentina and Brazil on as partners in "Operation Juarez." Failing that, in September 1982, López Portillo acted on LaRouche's proposal, adopting credit controls on Mexico's currency, nationalizing the Mexican banking system, and announcing a debt moratorium on Mexican debt. Wall Street, the City of London, and allied intelligence agencies, having scrambled to prevent implementation of LaRouche's plan, now targetted LaRouche and López Portillo. Nonetheless, in October 1982, in a speech at the UN, López Portillo called for a new finan-

LaRouche opponent Walter Raymond Smiles. The CIA's Walter Raymond, Jr., sits between President Reagan and his National Security Adviser, John Poindexter.

cial system essentially along the lines LaRouche had specified.

These proposals were all perfectly consistent with Franklin Delano Roosevelt's vision beyond World War II of ending British colonialism, and developing the world based upon reciprocally beneficial trade relationships among nation states, the "idealism" Henry Kissinger attacked in his Chatham House address.

Such were a few of Lyndon LaRouche's many activities in 1982.

1982-1983 were years of enormous battles within the Reagan Administration. On one side was National Security Adviser William Clark and his assistant Richard Morris, who continued to task LaRouche and his colleagues at *EIR* on national security issues. On the other were the Anglophiles controlled by Vice President Bush, who found LaRouche to be "the most dangerous man in America." Richard Morris testified in the LaRouche cases that Kenneth deGraffenreid, Walter Raymond, and Roy Godson were the three most vocal opponents of LaRouche inside the Reagan Administration. Raymond, along with Bush, deGraffenreid, and Margaret Thatcher, were the primary authors of Project Democracy, ceding perception-control and regime-change operations to private organizations and NGOs operating under CIA and MI6 direction.

Enter Mueller

In 1982, Robert Mueller joined the staff of U.S. Attorney William Weld in Boston, Massachusetts. He had previously been in private practice in San Francisco while waiting to be accepted into the U.S. Attorney's office there. His life's dream was to prosecute. Mueller and Weld concentrated on public corruption cases, targeting and taking down the administration of popular Boston Mayor Kevin White, in an investigation widely criticized for "gestapo tactics" and prosecutorial misconduct.

Following LaRouche's 1984 Presidential campaign and a public claim by Kissinger that LaRouche would be "dealt with" after the election, William Weld opened a criminal investigation of LaRouche's Presidential campaign committees, claiming that the campaign had engaged in credit card fraud. While there was a barrage of initial publicity, and companies associated with LaRouche suffered huge contempt fines because they refused to turn over to Weld's office information about their contributors, the investigation languished over the course of two years and two grand juries.

While the criminal investigation stalled, numerous classified counterintelligence investigations were launched, under Executive Order 12333, justifying surveillance prohibited by the Constitution's Fourth Amendment, infiltration, and classified counterintelligence "neutralization" tactics. These covert operations were used to create an otherwise non-existent criminal case. FOIA documents released over the years revealed a number of such classified operations based on fabricated assertions by government agents. Many of these operations remain classified to this day. In 1992 and 1993, investigators for LaRouche confirmed that the Leesburg offices of *EIR* and other LaRouche-associated entities were subject to intense warrantless surveillance conducted through NSA hubs in Northern Virginia's AT&T offices, and that numerous black-bag burglaries had been conducted through the local sheriff's office and Deputy Donald Moore.

Gage Skidmore

William Weld

In March 1986, two LaRouche Democrats, Mark Fairchild and Janice Hart, won the Illinois Democratic Primary for Lieutenant Governor and Secretary of State. They were part of a slate of over 1,000 LaRouche Democrats who ran for office that year. A huge, daily, national media defamation campaign followed, using the John Train playbook and many of the Train salon participants. The Boston investigation was revamped. Mueller, who succeeded William Weld as acting U.S. Attorney in 1986, after Weld decamped to Washington to head the Bush Justice Department's Criminal Division, brought in John J.E. Markham II to take the lead in the LaRouche investigation. Markham had been a member of the Process Church of the Final Judgment, a satanic cult tied to Charles Manson, during his early legal career. Plans for a search of offices associated with LaRouche in Leesburg and Boston were set into motion.

There were two plans for the Leesburg raid, one buried in official FBI documents, and the other hidden in secret communications. One of the raid's principals, Donald Moore, told an FBI informant in 1992 that a plan was in circulation weeks before the assault, to provoke LaRouche's security guards into a shooting incident by staging a massive siege and provocation at Ibykus Farm where LaRouche stayed. According to Moore, he had provided detailed plans for the eventuality of entering the farm and killing LaRouche. FBI case agent Richard Egan corroborated Moore's account, stating in court testimony that his activity

EIRNS/Stuart Lewis

John Markham

under the warrant consisted of a frantic search for evidence justifying a second search warrant for Ibykus Farm and an arrest warrant for LaRouche.

Utilizing what he has come to call "shock and awe" tactics, Mueller employed a force of some 400 law enforcement agents and privately owned armored personnel carriers to raid two office buildings in Leesburg, Virginia, where *EIR* and other companies associated with LaRouche were located—this, for what former Attorney General Ramsey Clark accurately describes as "book people." Ibykus Farm was surrounded by SWAT teams in black ninja gear, and helicopters flew overhead.

At 10 p.m, Fox News reported that authorities were about to enter Ibykus Farm to search for a "weapons cache." No such weapons cache existed, and the FBI and ATF knew it. The plan to kill LaRouche was only aborted when his associates sent a telegram to President Reagan seeking his intervention.

Based on a classified mechanism with the Joint Chiefs of Staff, documents seized in the raid were taken to a military facility, Henderson Hall, where they were undoubtedly reviewed by intelligence officials for purposes of their continued classified operations. William Weld, now heading the Department of Justice Criminal Division, claimed that this extraordinary procedure was necessary to prevent the LaRouche people from breaking into a normal government facility and stealing back their documents!

On the day of the raid, Mueller and Markham targeted and arrested key personnel involved in LaRouche's intelligence functions and security, charging them with obstruction of justice. To break them, the prosecutors sought lengthy periods of detention, which the Alexandria federal court granted based on the wave of poisonous publicity surrounding the raid, and numerous inflammatory and false statements to the court by John Markham. When those statements were later proved to be false, the defendants, now released, were without a real remedy except to call the Boston trial court's attention to Markham's lies.

At the same time, key prosecution witnesses underwent "deprogramming" by so-called cult experts to prepare for testimony, and were granted numerous benefits never disclosed to the defense. Markham and

EIRNS/Stuart Lewis

Raid on the Leesburg offices associated with Lyndon LaRouche, October 6, 1986.

Mueller employed the ADL for witness interviews, thus evading the requirements for disclosure required of government agents, used Dennis King as a consultant, and used inflammatory allegations which they knew to be false in television broadcasts aimed at poisoning the jury pool. Donald Moore, who had illegally burglarized *EIR*'s offices and mapped LaRouche's assassination, was invited by Markham and Mueller to come to Boston to serve as their assistant on the criminal case.

The Boston case, in which LaRouche was indicted for obstruction of justice, fell apart when FOIA documents revealed small aspects of the secret covert operations being run parallel to the criminal prosecution—notably a document from Ollie North's safe indicating extreme White House interest in players in the LaRouche case. As a result, Federal Judge Robert Keeton, following the classified trail, which he viewed in documents he ordered be presented to him *in camera*, ordered a search of Vice President Bush's office for exculpatory evidence. During prosecutorial misconduct hearings conducted before Judge Keeton, it was also discovered that a national security informant had been infiltrated into the LaRouche security operation, and that John Markham had instructed him to advise the defendants to obstruct justice, in words dictated by Markham, knowing that the defendants would write the informant's words down in their notebooks. The fabricated and planted notebook quotes were then used by Markham in his opening statement to the jury, as proof that the defendants had conspired to obstruct justice.

The lengthy government misconduct hearings Judge Keeton conducted resulted in a mistrial due to juror hardship. More troublesome for Mueller and Markham, jurors told the *Boston Herald* that they would have voted not guilty if the case had ended at that point, following testimony on the credit card fraud counts of the indictment. Judge Keeton found that the government had engaged in "systemic and institutional prosecutorial misconduct" in the case. In a separate opinion, he opened the door to further discovery of classified operations in a retrial, in order to allow the defendants to show that they did not have the "corrupt motive" necessary for an obstruction of justice conviction.

The Justice Department quickly opened a new massive LaRouche case before Judge Albert V. Bryan Jr. in Alexandria, Virginia, this time based on a conspiracy to commit loan fraud and a conspiracy to prevent the IRS from assessing taxes. LaRouche was the sole defendant charged in both of the two counts, and all defendants were convicted. Bryan raced the case from indictment to trial, preventing adequate defense preparation; invited the government to conceal evidence by denying all motions for exculpatory evidence; and prevented the defense from introducing the fact that the government had bankrupted the companies taking political loans, preventing them from repaying the political loans, in a case in which the government claimed loan fraud based on non-repayment of the same political loans. Judge Bryan himself had signed the order initiating the unprecedented government-instigated bankruptcy. U.S. Bankruptcy Judge Martin Bostetter later ruled that the bankruptcy was a "constructive fraud" on the court. Praising his railroad, Judge Bryan mocked Judge Keeton openly, saying Keeton "owed him a cigar" for "disposing" of the LaRouche matter.

Former U.S. Attorney General Ramsey Clark, who represented LaRouche on appeal, said that the La-Rouche case represented "a broader range of deliberate cunning and systemic misconduct over a longer period of time, using the power of the federal government, than any other prosecution by the U.S. government in my time or to my knowledge." After reviewing the federal cases during hearings held in his Court, widely respected New York Supreme Court Justice Stephen G. Crane found that the "actions of federal prosecutors raised an inference of a conspiracy to lay low these defendants at any cost."

Needless to say, Robert Mueller does not feature the LaRouche case as a career highlight.

Ascending the Bush Family Ladder

In 1989, George H.W. Bush brought Robert Mueller to Main Justice to dispose of another nemesis, Panamanian President Manuel Noriega. Aside from supporting LaRouche's "Operation Juarez," Noriega had refused to go along with the cocaine financing of George H.W. Bush's Contra insurgency operations directed at El Salvador and Nicaragua. Based on his work for the CIA, Noriega just knew way too much about George H.W. Bush and cocaine. Following multiple unsuccessful coup attempts against Noriega, more than 28,000 U.S. troops invaded Panama on Dec. 20,1989, killing hundreds of Panamanians, deposing Noriega's government and armed forces, and extracting Noriega for trial in the United States. The operation was dubbed "Operation Just Cause," an antonym if there ever was one.

Manual Noriega was known in the CIA and DEA as a steadfast drug fighter, and DEA and CIA agents testified to that fact at his trial. To overcome this problem, Mueller dealt Latin America's most notorious drug gangs "get out of jail free" cards as bribes, if they would say that Noriega dealt drugs. According to reporter Glenn Garvin, Mueller plea bargained down a potential 1,435 years in prison for the lying narcotrafficker criminals testifying for him, to 81 years. These deals and bribes included a $1.25 million bribe to members of the Cali Cartel (whose leaders Noriega had jailed) and a deal with self-avowed Hitler worshipper Carlos Lehder Rivas, leader of the Medellin Cartel. Once again, charges of prosecutorial misconduct flowed daily from Noriega's defense and appellate legal teams, but the media operations accompanying the prosecutions had turned Noriega into a devil whose claims did not deserve to be heard.

Having done the assignment on Noriega, Mueller ascended to head the Justice Department's Criminal Di-

President of Panama Manuel Noriega, in Panama, April 1988.

vision. Here he successfully covered up the drug, weapons, and terrorism activities of two banks, BCCI and BNL. BCCI was the Anglo-American intelligence community's chosen vehicle to fund terrorism, launder drug money, and fund dark intelligence activities in Afghanistan, Central America, and throughout the Middle East. The highest levels of the British and European oligarchies were directly implicated in BCCI's activities. Both banks escaped with plea bargains and fines, protecting dirty state secrets on several continents from public disclosure. Mueller left the Justice Department in 1993 for private practice, a stint in Washington D.C.'s Homicide Division, and then a stint as U.S. Attorney for the Northern District of California in San Francisco.

Based on family services rendered, President George W. Bush returned Mueller to Main Justice as acting Deputy Attorney General in the early days of his Administration, before appointing him, in July of 2001, to head the FBI. He assumed that office on Sept. 4, 2001, only days before Sept. 11. As we shall see, he played a commanding role in covering up for the perpetrators of the murder of nearly 3,000 Americans on that date, while overseeing the creation of the police state measures which followed that attack.

Aggressive Deception of the American People Concerning 9/11

There is a picture formerly available from the Bush Presidential Library which shows George W. Bush, Dick Cheney, Condoleezza Rice, and Prince Bandar, Saudi Arabia's U.S. Ambassador, on the White House balcony two days after September 11, 2001. The men are smoking cigars. Reporters inquiring about the photo more recently have been told it is no longer available from the Bush Library.[2] Maybe the picture in this case says more than a thousand words ever could. Again, two days after almost 3,000 Americans were murdered by 19 hijackers, 15 of whom were Saudis, the Saudi Ambassador yucks it up with the President, Dick Cheney, and the National Security Adviser on the White House balcony.

Immediately after September 11, 2001, Bandar arranged for a mass exodus of Saudi royals, intelligence personnel, and other Saudi nationals from the United States, including members of the bin Laden family, with the full cooperation of the United States government. He placed them beyond the reach of any future inquiry.

It is obvious that the 9/11 terrorists did not emerge out of bat caves in Afghanistan. They lived here in the United States, training for a suicide mission which required massive logistical support. The immediate conclusion of anyone thinking through the plot, is that this had to be state-sponsored terrorism. The Bush Administration, however, immediately focused the nation on Iraq and took the nation to a disastrous war there, when even the most basic common sense told investigators to focus initially on the Saudis, following the evidence from there.

Congress convened a Joint Congressional Inquiry into the events of 9/11 in 2002, chaired by then U.S. Senator Bob Graham. Senator Graham says that he has stopped using the term "cover-up" in relation to 9/11. He instead uses the term "aggressive deception," and places Mueller, operating on behalf of the Bush family, at the center of obstructing his investigation and others. It was Mueller who angrily intervened to prevent Congressional investigators from visiting FBI offices in San Diego. They went anyway, and discovered troves of FBI documents concerning the Saudi hijackers' San Diego cell, and its support by Saudi royals and government officials, which Mueller's FBI never made available to the Congressional inquiry, despite their specific requests.

Prince Bandar, so close to the Bush family that he was called "Bandar Bush," is at the center of the sup-

---

2. The photo is available from History Commons.

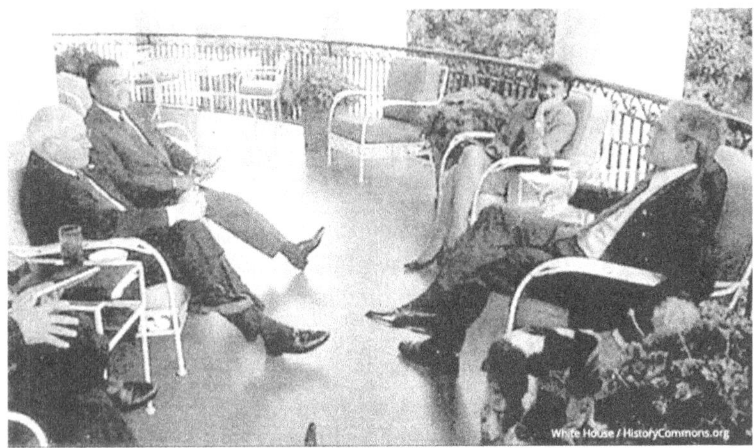

White House

Saudi Prince Bandar at the White House. From left, Dick Cheney, Prince Bandar, Condoleezza Rice, and President George W. Bush, Sept. 13, 2001.

port network for the San Diego hijackers. There were multiple documents in the San Diego FBI files referencing well-known sympathies for Al-Qaeda by employees of the Saudi embassy in D.C., including Osama Bin Laden's half-brother. There were records of checks paid to Saudis supporting the two San Diego hijackers from Bandar's wife. There was also a CIA memorandum carefully tracking Saudi government support for Al-Qaeda and other Saudi terrorist organizations.

Congressional investigators also discovered the identity of an FBI informant who was close to both San Diego hijackers and rented rooms to them, living in the same house. Rather than allowing investigators to interview the informant, Mueller placed him in an FBI safehouse for "his protection."

The results of the Joint Congressional Inquiry's review of Saudi government support of the 9/11 hijackers, 28 pages of the Joint Congressional Committee's report, were classified in the final report. They remained classified, despite the demands of the 9/11 families and an all-out national campaign for their release, until July 15, 2016. According to all concerned, the man who classified these 28 pages in 2003—and adamantly fought to ensure that they would never see the light of day—was FBI Director Robert Mueller. The 28 pages solely concern what Congressional investigators found in the San Diego FBI office, the discovery of which Robert Mueller actively sought to prevent.

In the summer of 2015, another document formerly classified, Document 17, was quietly declassified. It was authored by the same Congressional investigators who wrote the 28 pages, and revealed that two Saudi students, funded by the Saudi government, did a dry run

of the September 11, 2001 attack on an American West flight from Phoenix to Washington in 1999, an incident well-known to the FBI. After releasing the two Saudis from custody, the FBI subsequently learned, in 2000, that one of the students had been trained in Afghanistan's Al-Qaeda camps to conduct Khobar Towers type assaults, and the other was tied to terrorist elements as well.

Senator Graham has remarked that Mueller stone-walled his investigation at every turn. Undoubtedly, large volumes of documents concerning the Saudi role in 9/11 reside in still classified and undisclosed CIA, FBI, and other files.

This is not the place for a full review of the joint British and American responsibility for Salafist terrorism. From the U.S. side, Zbigniew Brzezinski deliberately created and supported an entire generation of such terrorists, including Osama bin Laden, in his geopolitical war game with the Soviet Union. He deliberately created a terrorist insurgency in Afghanistan in order to draw the Russians into a war there, and gloated about it until his recent death. Saudi Arabia has never been anything other than a satrapy of the British, and the second incubation point for the terrorist phenomena manifesting themselves in 9/11 lies in the mosques of "Londonistan." The CIA knew this. MI6 knew this. They had been using these terrorist networks for years for their own geopolitical purposes.

The FBI did not pay attention to the Saudis before 2001 because "they were an ally," according to testimony provided in the wake of the attacks. In August 2001, President Bush was handed a CIA briefing which explicitly warned that Al-Qaeda was about to launch a major attack on the United States using airplanes. The President did nothing. Earlier, Robert Mueller, serving as Deputy Attorney General in the days prior to 9/11, had blocked a major funding increase for the FBI's counter-terrorism division led by John O'Neill. O'Neill had moved his entire operation to New York because official Washington would not listen to his warnings about Al-Qaeda. The job to "aggressively deceive" the American people about this sordid history fell to Robert Swan Mueller III, and he obstructed a Congressional investigation to do precisely that.

Due to an act of Congress, JASTA, the 9/11 families are now proceeding with their lawsuit against the Saudis. But why should they have to endure years more of litigation? Why doesn't President Trump open the actual door on this process, assigning seasoned investigators, like Michael Jacobsen, who unearthed the San Diego FBI trove, to a full review and disclosure of the Saudi role in 9/11, the U.S. and British government role in creating and fostering Islamic terrorism, and the "aggressive deception" and obstruction of justice by Robert Mueller and others which resulted in this illegal coverup?

While engaged in "aggressive deception" about the criminal conspiracy resulting in almost 3,000 American murders, Robert Mueller continued to railroad innocents. He personally directed the PENTBOM investigation which falsely accused Dr. Steven Hatfill of mailing the deadly Anthrax letters which killed five people in 2001. For years, Mueller harassed the innocent Dr. Hatfill, ordering the FBI to search his apartment multiple times, searching the apartment of his girlfriend, ensuring that Hatfill lost his job, and leaking continuously to the national news media about Hatfill's alleged perfidies. Once, when an FBI agent ran over Hatfill's foot with his car, it was arranged that Hatfill would get a ticket for impeding traffic. The Justice Department finally paid Hatfill $5.8 million dollars to settle his Privacy Act lawsuit aimed at government leaks—a settlement, along with an exoneration, which only came when a federal judge insisted that reporters reveal their Justice Department and FBI sources for stories about Hatfill.

As part of the same PENTBOM 9/11 investigation which destroyed Hatfill's life, Mueller, with Attorney General John Ashcroft, rounded up 762 Muslims who had overstayed their visas, and were identified via tips to the FBI "tip line" from a hysterical public reacting to the events of 9/11. Remember, Prince Bandar had already moved the key Saudis involved with the hijackers out of the United States. These individuals were detained, without charges, in a special unit of New York's Metropolitan Detention Center. Their jail conditions were supervised by Mueller and a small group of other Washington officials, and amounted to torture. They were deprived of sleep and food, repeatedly strip searched, physically and verbally abused by guards, and denied basic hygiene items like soap, toilet paper, and towels, or any access to the outside world. Both the U.S. District Court for the Eastern District of New York and the Second Circuit kept Mueller as a defendant in the subsequent civil rights suit brought by the detainees. This means, under the high standard of proof required of civil rights plaintiffs, that the judges were literally appalled by the allegations against Robert Mueller in the complaint. In a 4-2 decision on June 18, 2017, however, the Supreme Court let the newly appointed Special Prosecutor out of the lawsuit. Here is what Justice Stephen Breyer said in his dissent:

> The majority opinion well summarizes the particular claims that the plaintiffs make in this suit. All concern the conditions of their confinement, which began soon after the September 11, 2001 attacks and lasted for days and weeks, then stretching into months. At some point, *all the defendants knew that they had nothing to do with the September 11 attacks but continued to detain them anyway under harsh conditions*. Official government policy, both before and after the defendants became aware of the plaintiffs' innocence led to the plaintiffs being held in "tiny cells for over 23 hours a day, with lights continuously left on, shackled when moved, often strip searched, and denied access to most forms of communication with the outside world." The defendants detained the plaintiffs in these conditions on the basis of their race or religion and without justification.

Mueller is often touted by the Washington establishment for reorganizing the FBI to become an effective counterintelligence and counterterrorism organization in the wake of 9/11. This also is Washington D.C. public relations claptrap. The FBI under Mueller excelled at entrapping the otherwise innocent, and constructing a surveillance state strongly resembling that portrayed by George Orwell in the novel, *1984.* In the Newburgh Four case, for example, the presiding judge said the FBI, "came up with the crime, provided the means, and removed all relevant obstacles, making a terrorist out of a man whose buffoonery is positively Shakespearean in scope."

Studies have found that almost every domestic terrorist plot during Mueller's tenure, from 2001 to 2010, was in some way cooked up, assisted, and eventually busted by Mueller's FBI. The book, *The Terror Factory—Inside the FBI's Manufactured War on Terrorism* by Trevor Aaronson, documents this in chilling detail. J. Edgar Hoover's domestic security depravities seem pale in comparison.

The FBI now manages some 15,000 designated informants through a Linked-In type data base called Delta. It allows FBI agents to dial up informants to use

Robert Mueller and George W. Bush.

in stings anywhere in the country. Informants then travel to their assignments and can earn up to $100,000 for entrapping and testifying against the unwary petty criminals, losers, and mentally-challenged individuals who inhabit the Bureau's terrorist case docket. Philip Mudd was brought over from the CIA by Mueller to lead this effort in the FBI's new National Security Division. Mudd, using a data-mining system called Domain Management, flooded immigrant communities, particularly Muslim communities, with informants to monitor and entrap those who expressed ideas favorable to radical Islam, whether or not those expressing the ideas had any real possibility of ever engaging in a terrorist plot. FBI agents referred to the Mudd-Mueller surveillance and entrapment tools as "battlefield management." In other words, entire communities in the United States have been targeted and treated to the methods of the East German Stasi. On Aug. 10, 2017, Mudd, now a CNN "analyst" who has raved repeatedly against President Donald Trump, told CNN analyst Jake Tapper, that the U.S. government "is going to kill this guy," meaning the President.

Then, there is the surveillance state. William Binney was the most senior-technical analyst at the NSA. He designed a system, "ThinThread," which would accurately track terrorist plots while preserving the civil liberties of American citizens. In the film, The *Good American*, Binney tells the story of how he did this, and how General Michael Hayden, then the Director of the

NSA, ditched Binney's program and spent millions of dollars with an outside contractor, SAIC, on an alternative system, Trailblazer, which mass-collected data on every American, in violation of the Fourth Amendment. Drowning in data under SAIC's alternative surveillance program, the NSA was unable to pinpoint actual terrorist plots. Binney and his collaborators demonstrated that under his program, ThinThread, all of the information necessary to stop the 9/11 hijackers was recorded by the NSA and readily available to investigators. For that, Robert Mueller sent the FBI to raid and harass Binney and his collaborators, bringing criminal charges against one of them, Thomas Drake, which were later dropped.

And then, of course, there is Enron, another notch in Mueller's prosecutorial belt. Stretching the law on obstruction of justice, Mueller and his task force went after Arthur Andersen & Company, then one of the world's largest accounting firms, for the perfidies of Enron, charging the accountants with obstruction of justice. The U.S. Supreme Court found that Mueller and friends had stretched the obstruction statute beyond recognition to prevail in the case, a reversal which came too late for the company and the people who worked there. Arthur Andersen went out of business as a result of Mueller's prosecution.

The True Origins of the Coup Against the President

The coup against Donald Trump, in which Robert Mueller has been assigned to conduct the concluding acts, actually began in 2013-2014. The popular explanation for the perfidies and crimes against the President is that Hillary Clinton and Barack Obama employed their networks, including stay-behind loyalists in the government and in the intelligence community, to change the result of the U.S. election, to stage the ongoing coup. This explanation, focused primarily on events in 2016, while true in an immediate domestic sense, misses the larger picture. As we shall show, the British starting calling for Donald Trump's head, by their own account, in 2015 and meddled and meddled in the U.S. election and the coup to reverse its result every day thereafter. A recent book by Dick Morris and Ellen

McGann, *Rogue Spooks, the Intelligence War on Trump*, puts appropriate emphasis on the British origin of the war against the President, but assigns the wrong motive for the crimes committed.

Why, for example, did the FBI obtain a FISA warrant for Paul Manafort in 2014 based on his political consulting work in Ukraine? Why, according to accounts in the *Guardian,* did the British start demanding Trump's head in 2015, and warn that the DNC computers had been hacked in July of 2015, a full year before the DNC alleged it had been hacked? Why did the British keep pushing and pushing for Trump's removal by any means necessary? Why was Hillary Clinton's campaign working not only with British intelligence's Michael Steele and Sir Andrew Wood to develop dirt on Trump, but also with Ukrainian intelligence? Why was NATO intelligence, an appendage of the British, raving about Russian bots and Russian "hybrid warfare," leaking repeatedly to the London press in 2014 and 2015 about the purported evil emanating from the St. Petersburg Internet Research Agency and thousands of paid Internet trolls?

The Real Story: Issues of War, Peace, and the Future

Beginning with an announcement of President Xi Jinping, at a conference in Kazakhstan in July 2013, China has set into motion an entirely new dynamic in the world, a new paradigm of cooperation between nation states, to build vital modern infrastructure allowing nations in the former "developing sector" to reach their full economic potentials. Xi Jinping's vision of the New Silk Road or "One Belt, One Road" project has been endorsed by Russia's Vladimir Putin. Russia and China are joining in projects which will fully develop the Eurasian landmass, creating a "new financial architecture" in the Asia-Pacific region.

On July 16, 2014, the BRICS group of nations meeting in Fortaleza, Brazil, joined by the Latin American heads of state, agreed with Xi Jinping's proposal on the creation of an entirely new economic and financial system, representing a fundamental alternative to the casino economy of the present system of globalization. The Anglo-American globalist system is based on maximized profit of the few, and the impoverishment of billions of people. In the new paradigm, financing for joint great projects is to come from development banks, such as the newly created Asian Infrastructure Investment Bank, ending dependence on such globalist institutions as the IMF or World Bank. Globalization as administered by the IMF and World Bank is effectively a system of imperial debt slavery, keeping the nations dependent on their loans in primitive economic conditions, while their raw materials are looted.

As Prime Minister Narenda Modi of India remarked, "The BRICS is unique as an international institution. In this first instance, it unifies a group of nations, not on the basis of their existing prosperity or common identities, but rather their future potentials. The idea of the BRICS itself is thus aligned with the future." It is not incidental to this remark that Russia, China, and India have set future goals for space exploration, including most specifically exploration of the Moon and possible exploitation of Helium 3 on the Moon, which has the potential of finally realizing nuclear fusion power as a primary energy source powering the world.

China has made clear that no small part of this initiative is inspired by the work of Lyndon and Helga LaRouche. Many of the envisioned projects reflect longstanding proposals by *Executive Intelligence Review* and the Schiller Institute. The methods employed echo the ideas of political economy first developed by Alexander Hamilton, and deployed by Abraham Lincoln and Franklin Roosevelt—ideas uniquely developed and expanded by Lyndon LaRouche. Xi Jinping has asked the United States to join this great venture, which could produce thousands of productive jobs and jump-start infrastructure projects in this country. Obama adamantly refused Xi's offer, and did everything in his power to block and defeat the Chinese initiative. President Trump has indicated an openness to the proposition.

These 2013-2014 events were and are a direct challenge to the British imperial system. They directly challenge the monetary system which is the source of Anglo-American domination of the world. They directly challenge fundamental British strategic policy extant since the days of Halford Mackinder. Under the "One Belt, One Road" initiative, joined with Russia's Eurasian Union, Mackinder's "world island" of Eurasia and Africa will be developed, crisscrossed with new high-speed rail links, new cities, and vital modern infrastructure, based on the mutual benefit of all of the nation states existing there. Under the British geopolitical model, this area of the world has been subjected to endless instability, war, and raw materials looting. Xi Jinping has also attacked the geopolitical axioms by which the United States and the British have operated. He proposes instead a model of "win-win" cooperation

Victoria Nuland, of President Obama's State Department, hands out cookies to ground troops of the color revolution in Kiev, 2014.

Nixon committed proven crimes) paled in comparison to Russia-gate (where both Clapper and Comey have testified that, to date, the President has committed no crimes). In addition, Clapper told the Aussies to target China, accusing the Chinese, without any offer of proof, of meddling in Australia's elections. Former FBI Director James Comey backed Clapper in his testimony on June 8, 2017, attempting to wax eloquent in response to Senator Joe Manchin, about how Putin exists with one purpose in mind—to shred and dismember the United States.

But China and Russia have completely outflanked these cretins, and the new paradigm is rapidly coming to life with "shovels in the ground" everywhere. In response, the Anglo-American elites have absolutely nothing to offer the world except the same dying, decadent globalist "order." This explains why many in official Washington let loose their inner alien monster every time the President mentions a desire for better relations with Russia, or evinces his friendship with President Xi Jinping of China. This is why Hillary Clinton has literally gone insane, raving like Lady Macbeth, and obsessing about Putin's "man-spreading." That is why, also, they would risk World War III rather than see the "Belt and Road," the New Silk Road, go forward with its "community of principle" idea of relations among nations.

in which nation states collaborate for development based on the common aims of mankind.

The Anglo-American response to this development can be seen in the events in Ukraine, where Obama, the British, and the National Endowment for Democracy staged a coup in February 2014, overthrowing the government of the duly elected President, Victor Yanukovych, because he refused to turn his country into a western satrapy to be wielded against Putin's Russia. Assistant Secretary of State for European and Eurasian Affairs Victoria Nuland, who helped oversee the coup from her perch at Hillary Clinton's State Department, was famously caught on tape dictating the Ukraine succession, after bands of murderous neo-Nazis did the scut-work for the coup. According to Nuland, the price for this handiwork was some $5 billion.

The actual "swamp" of the British and their accomplices in the U.S. intelligence community and aligned trans-Atlantic institutions, like NATO, have viewed themselves as being in a state of war against Russia and China since the 2013-2014 events. Think about former DNI Clapper's unhinged speech of June 7, 2017 in Australia. Clapper ranted that it was in Putin's and Russia's "genes" to attack the United States. Since Trump pursues better relations and shared intelligence with Russia on terrorism, Clapper ranted, Watergate (where Richard

What Did Trump Do?

Like LaRouche, Trump represents an existential challenge to the post-War British-dictated monetarist and imperial order. In his campaign platform he called for the reinstitution of Glass-Steagall banking separation. This would end the casino economy which is about to blow up again—the real economy never having recovered from the collapse of 2008. He wants to build huge modern infrastructure and revitalize the manufacturing sector of the economy with modern manufacturing techniques. He wants to return the United States to space exploration and the funding of fundamental science, recognizing the optimistic national morale which will result from that.

In his public speeches, Trump has repeatedly invoked what he understands as "The American System" of political economy, a concept developed and elaborated in recent history by only one man, Lyndon LaRouche. This centers economic systems in nation states, rather than global institutions, and calls for harnessing the resources of the nation state to develop the economy to higher and higher levels of physical productivity and human culture. While Trump has features in his version of the American System which LaRouche would not endorse as historically accurate or politically wise, even the use of the term, invoking Alexander Hamilton and Lincoln's economist Henry Carey, is a direct challenge to the free trade, small-government nostrums foisted on the United States by a parade of British agents during the Twentieth Century.

The British, up to this point, have been largely successful in burying the actual ideas of Alexander Hamilton and Franklin Roosevelt, and burying the fundamental advances in these ideas resulting from original discoveries by LaRouche. Through deliberate miseducation of Americans, the British have made their economic theories and systems, against which Americans explicitly fought in our Revolution, appear to be universal laws of human behavior.

UN Photo/Cia Pak

U.S. President Donald Trump addresses the UN General Assembly, Sept. 19, 2017.

As his Sept. 19 speech to the United Nations emphasized, Trump envisions a system of sovereign nations, each striving to develop and enrich their populations, engaged in cooperative trade relationships, reciprocal in nature and targeted for the benefit of each party. His U.N. speech echoed the foreign policy of John Quincy Adams, a policy which forbade our nation from "going abroad, seeking monsters to destroy." This is the very opposite of the imperial-gendarme, perpetual-war policy long favored by the British for the United States. Trump's positive vision, under present circumstances, requires active collaboration with Russia and China.

To stop the coup, the President's team and his supporters must stop reacting defensively. He must act on the aspects of his program—Glass-Steagall, large scale infrastructure development funded by national banking mechanisms devoted to that purpose, space exploration, fusion power development, and joining the "One Belt, One Road" program with China, which can actually save the economy and produce high paying jobs. At the same time, they should look at the actual crimes involved in the coup which are already on the public record, investigate them—including in the Congress— and prosecute them. With respect to Mueller, they should investigate his obstruction of the investigation into the crimes committed on 9/11, together with a full public unveiling of the Saudi and British role in international terrorism. In aid of such an effort we present seven crimes implicated in the events in the coup against the President to date.

Seven Actual Crimes

The seven crimes outlined below make clear that a Special Counsel, not Robert Swan Mueller III, should be investigating the events prior to June 2016. The subject of the investigation is that a foreign power has been instigating an insurrection in the U.S.

In the British account of the 2016 American election, largely published in pieces in the *Guardian*, they began warning their American counterparts about the dangers of Donald Trump's accommodating views toward Putin and Russia in 2015. These warnings were followed by the specific claim that the Democratic National Committee's servers had been hacked by the Russians as of July 2015. According to the British account, their American counterparts were slow to respond, although the FBI says it notified the DNC, which did nothing about the alleged Russian hack until June 2016.

The obvious should be stated here. If the British were developing dossiers on Trump and his associates as early as 2015, Trump and his associates were under surveillance as of that date or sooner by British GCHQ and/or the NSA. We know that Paul Manafort was considered practically an enemy combatant in Anglo-American swamp circles by 2014, because of his Ukraine work with Yanukovych and the Party of the Regions. He apparently chose the wrong side by fighting against a Nazi coup. The same was true even of Democratic consultants such as Tony Podesta, who worked with Manafort on Ukraine and were subject to the same reported 2014 FISA surveillance warrant. What was the FBI affidavit which justified the 2014 Manafort and Podesta FISA court surveillance warrant, and what was the British role in obtaining it? What role did the British play, including GCHQ and MI6, in the Manafort counterintelligence investigation? What were the British "concerns" about Trump communicated to U.S. intelligence as early as 2015? What was the specific British warning about hacks of the DNC computer in July 2015?

By December 2015, according to James Clapper's dodgy January 2017 report on alleged Russian meddling in the election, hundreds of paid Russian trolls associated with the St. Petersburg, Russia, Internet Research Agency had begun to advocate for Trump's election. At the same time, Michael Flynn attended a dinner at *RT* in Russia, sitting across the table from Putin. Flynn had already driven Obama crazy by proposing a determined U.S.-Russian collaboration in the war on terror, and going after the Administration's policy aimed at dismembering Syria. Obama had fired him. Is this the date when surveillance on Flynn actually began, or did it begin sooner? What was the British role in this surveillance?

Carter Page has also been a subject in Mueller's Russiagate hysteria. He apparently walked in to volunteer for the Trump campaign without any prior association with the President, and was disavowed by the campaign soon after. He went to school in London, had a variety of business dealings in Russia, and had volunteered for the Trump campaign as a foreign policy advi-

sor by simply walking in the door. Page had already functioned as an FBI informant in a major 2013 New York City FBI case against Russian organized crime figures, and stated on CNN that he briefed both the CIA and FBI regularly on these business dealings in Russia. Was he used as a front to get a FISA warrant directed at the Trump campaign? Was he a spy sent by the FBI both to Russia and into the Trump campaign?

The targeting of the alleged activities of the St. Petersburg Internet Research Agency (IRA) in DNI Clapper's January report, again points to the heavy British hand in the coup against the President. According to French journalist Thierry Meyssan, in September 2014, the British government created the 77th Brigade, a unit tasked with countering foreign propaganda, which worked with the U.S. military in Europe *to interfere* with websites considered to be distributing Russian propaganda. This project ultimately morphed into NATO's Strategic Communications Service, tasked with suppressing any news or person favorable to the Russian position concerning strategic topics, but particularly Ukraine. From its inception, the NATO Strategic Communications Service incorporated a service of the Atlantic Council, the Digital Forensics Service. CrowdStrike's Dmitri Alperovitch—the person with sole access to the DNC's allegedly "hacked" computers, whose forensic analysis was adopted wholesale by James Comey's FBI and the U.S. intelligence community—is a senior fellow in the Atlantic Council's Digital Forensic Service.

News about Russian trolls operating out of the IRA and poisoning the Western mind filled the British press in 2015. In line with this NATO project is the Information Warfare Initiative in the U.S., centered at the Washington Center for European Policy Analysis and founded by *Washington Post* neo-con Anne Applebaum. It is a pseudopod of the National Endowment for Democracy and the U.S. intelligence community, and has concentrated its attacks on the Russian broadcasters RT and Sputnik.[3]

---

3. Russian trolls and IRA became a hot topic in Washington for the first time as a result of Clapper's reference to them in his January 2017 Assessment of Russian meddling, and a nationally embarrassing Senate Select Committee on Intelligence hearing in March 2017. There, full grown U.S. Senators listened in seemingly amazed wonder and without any challenge, as Thomas Rid, of King's College London and NATO, Roy Godson, and other British schooled intelligence experts wove a fantastic fairy tale. They told the Senators that thousands of paid Russian trolls using sophisticated bots had infiltrated the American mind with Russian generated conspiracy theories and swung the election to

Dmitri Alperovitch, co-founder and chief technology officer of CrowdStrike.

What exactly was the relationship of the *New York Times*, the *Washington Post*, CNN, and the other black propagandists operating against the President, together with their reporters, with the NED, the Information Warfare Initiative, NATO's Strategic Communications Service, and The Institute for Modern Russia in New York City, or other British or U.S. intelligence agencies during the Obama Administration and subsequently? Like the John Train meetings targeting LaRouche, the media attacks on the President are not organic. They are organized, and on a much larger scale than anything ever experienced in this country. What is the relationship of various Washington D.C. lobby shops, such as Orion Strategies, long associated with Senator John McCain, to the organized media campaign against Donald Trump? *Have our intelligence agencies actually instigated an Active Measures counterintelligence program illegally and against a sitting President?* What is the overlap of offices, personnel, and entities assigned by Obama to Russian, Chinese, and Eurasian intelligence functions, including the coup activities in Ukraine, with the illegal leaks of classified information to the news media?

Donald Trump. Godson repeatedly had to correct himself, substituting the current "Russia" for his constant reference to the Soviet Union. According to the same dubious sources, a second evil front opened by the crafty Russians consisted of purchase of Facebook ads meant to sow discord throughout our land.

The Cardinal Events of June-July 2016

1. The Conspiracy Against the President Takes Off

Sometime in June 2016, Hillary Clinton's campaign took over an opposition research project on Donald Trump which had previously been funded by Trump's Republican opponents. The contract was with a D.C. firm called Fusion GPS, which, in turn, employed a British firm, Orbis, and Orbis' founder Christopher Steele. Steele ran the Russia desk for MI6 until 2009; Sir Andrew Wood, an "associate" at Steele's company, was the British Ambassador to Moscow between 1995 and 2000, a "Russia" adviser to Tony Blair, and is an associate fellow of the Russia and Eurasia program at the Royal Institute of International Affairs at Chatham House. Christopher Burrows, Steele's partner in Orbis, lists himself as a long-time, high-ranking British foreign service officer, although news accounts also place him in British intelligence.

Christopher Steele has also acknowledged a long-standing relationship with the FBI, centered in the FBI's Eurasian Organized Crime Strike Force in New York City, which media reports date to 2010, the same time the relationship with Fusion GPS went into effect. Andrew McCabe, the ethically challenged FBI Assistant Director now being investigated for Hatch Act and other violations concerning the Clinton sponsorship of his wife's campaign against Virginia Senator Richard Black, led the Eurasian task force early in his career, and has maintained contacts ever since. Many believe that McCabe was Steele's FBI handler and contact.

In court filings in a London libel suit against them, Steele and Orbis state that they briefed reporters from the *New York Times*, the *Washington Post*, the *New Yorker*, Yahoo News, and CNN about Christopher Steele's reports on Trump and Russia in September 2016, and participated in further briefings with the *New York Times*, the *Washington Post*, and Yahoo News in October 2016. In late October, Steele briefed a reporter from *Mother Jones* via Skype. Senator John McCain and David Kramer, who was McCain's agent, were briefed on the pre-election Steele memoranda in December 2016. Sixteen memoranda smearing Trump, based on paid and anonymous Russian sources, were produced prior to the election. It is clear that the FBI was also a recipient of all of these memoranda dating back to June 2016, if not earlier.

Christopher Burrows (above), Christopher Steele's partner in Orbis, is a high-ranking British foreign service officer. FBI Assistant Director Andrew McCabe (right) is believed to be Steele's handler.

Steele and Orbis claim that the 17th memo, produced in December 2016, which referenced the salacious and disgusting claim that Trump engaged in perverse sexual activities at a Russian hotel, was solely produced to one David Kramer as a representative of John McCain, Senator John McCain himself, and a representative of the British security services. The December memo was the product of a collaboration between Steele, Sir Andrew Wood, Kramer, and a representative of the British security services, which began on November 18, 2016, that is, almost immediately following Trump's election as President. It has been widely reported that James Comey's FBI was also offering Steele and Orbis $50,000 or more at this point to corroborate aspects of the dodgy dossier smearing the President-elect.

David Kramer is the former President of the CIA and NED quango, Freedom House, was a fellow of the neo-conservative Project for a New American Century, held State Department positions dedicated to Project Democracy and soft power coups in Russia and the former East Bloc, and presently serves as Senior Director for Human Rights and Human Freedoms at Senator McCain's Institute for International Leadership in Arizona.

Hillary Clinton used the Steele dossier to paint Trump as a Russian dupe throughout her general election campaign against him. James Comey used it to justify his FBI counterintelligence probe of the Trump campaign which began in July 2016, and has continued.

Thus, we have the British government and, in all probability, NATO, intervening in an election in the United States to sway the result. Most certainly this raises questions about the applicability of election laws which bar foreign funding for exactly the reason that United States elections should be decided by United States citizens. Most certainly, once this sequence of events is fully investigated, it will become clear that all government participants intended to sway the election unlawfully, using the powers of a state to vanquish the will of the voters.

2. The Russian Hack That Wasn't—False Reporting of a Crime

On June 12, 2016, WikiLeaks announced that it was in possession of emails damaging to Hillary Clinton, and would soon be publishing them. June 14, 2016 marks the announcement by the Democratic National Committee that its computers had been hacked by the Russians, the subject apparently of the initial Christopher Steele memorandum prepared for the Clinton campaign. The purloined DNC emails showed, definitively, that the DNC, which should have been neutral in the primaries, was trying to destroy the rising campaign of Bernie Sanders. The emails were published by WikiLeaks on the eve of the Democratic National Convention. The claim that the WikiLeaks emails were the result of a Russian hack of DNC servers was authored by Dmitri Alperovitch of the security firm, Crowd Strike. Alperovitch, a Russian-American who demonizes Putin, is, as previously referenced, a fellow at the Atlantic Council's Digital Forensics Project, deeply involved in NATO's Strategic Communications Service.

The FBI's James Comey accepted Alperowitz's forensic analysis without ever accessing the DNC computers in question. It is probable that Comey was already operating on the basis of the British Christopher Steele memoranda asserting that the Russians were responsible for the DNC hack.

On July 24, 2017, the Veterans Intelligence Professionals for Sanity released a Memo to the President demonstrating that there was no Russian hack of the DNC. Rather, the WikiLeaks document trove was produced by a leak from inside the DNC, not a hack. According to this memorandum, the leaked treasure trove from the DNC was altered in a "cut and paste" job to

Gage Skidmore

Congressman Dana Rohrabacher recently met with Julian Assange of WikiLeaks.

make it look like it was the product of a very crude Russian hack. The VIPS are veterans of U.S. intelligence agencies, and include William Binney, the former technical director of the NSA. Their group first formed to oppose the fabricated reasons for the Iraq War. You can see the full interview of former CIA Officer Ray McGovern about the VIPS report here.

William Binney has insisted, from the first reference to Russian hacking as the source of the WikiLeaks Podesta/DNC documents, that if such an event had occurred, the NSA would have traced it and could say so with certainty. In their report, the VIPS point out that the CIA's Marble Framework program can obfuscate the source of cyberattacks and ceate false flag attribution to other state actors.

WikiLeaks has consistently claimed that the source of its dossier was an inside leak from the DNC, implying that Seth Rich, a DNC data management staffer who supported Bernie Sanders, was one of its sources. Rich was murdered in July 2016 in Washington, D.C., in a crime which remains unsolved at this date. Congressman Dana Rohrbacher (R-CA) recently met with Julian Assange of WikiLeaks, and states that Assange has evidence confirming that the WikiLeaks DNC/John Podesta email trove was the result of a leak, not a Russian hack.

3. The Trump Tower Meeting—Entrapping a Presidential Campaign

On June 9, 2016, a meeting took place in Trump Tower involving Donald Trump, Jr.; Paul Manafort, at the time the campaign manager for the Trump Presidential campaign; Jared Kushner, the President's son-in-law; and five other people. As opposed to media accounts, only one of the participants in the Trump Tower meeting was a Russian, the lawyer Natalia Veselnitskaya. By all accounts provided by participants, the meeting was very short, and involved the Magnitsky Act sanctions imposed by the U.S. Congress on certain Russians. Many consider these 2012 sanctions to be the opening shot of the New Cold War. This meeting has attracted extensive attention from Special Counsel Mueller, as the media have painted it as a "smoking gun."

The emails setting up the meeting do not reflect what actually happened at the meeting. Instead, they bear all the marks of an intelligence-agency entrapment attempt against Donald Trump, Jr., designed to fix the "Manchurian candidate" label on Trump early in the general election campaign. The emails setting up the meeting specifically offered "dirt" on Hillary Clinton to be provided by the Russian government itself.

On July 15, 2016, at the same time as the FBI was opening an investigation of the Russians for interfering in the U.S. election and of the Trump campaign for colluding with them, another British intelligence operative, Bill Browder, was filing a complaint with the U.S. Department of Justice concerning four participants in the Trump Tower meeting and others for failure to register under the Foreign Agents Registration Act. Browder's complaint claimed that these people were engaged in unregistered Russian lobbying activities, namely, attempting to overturn the Magnitsky Act. Browder renounced his American citizenship in 1989 to become a British subject and has operated at the highest levels of British finance and intelligence.

Undoubtedly, by the time of the June 9, 2016 Trump Tower meeting, the British government's Trump file already included a full history of Donald Trump's sponsorship of the 2013 Miss Universe pageant in Moscow and its players, Trump's real estate dealings with Russians anywhere in the world, all of candidate Trump's conciliatory statements toward Russia, and complaints that campaign advisor Michael Flynn was soft on Russia and a rebel against the U.S. intelligence establishment from within that establishment. The file also included surveillance of Trump's campaign manager, Paul Manafort, who was considered an outright enemy of Anglo-American interests given his political work for the former President of Ukraine, Victor Yanukovych and his Party of the Regions, and Trump's relationship with Felix Sater, a

Russian-American and high level FBI informant.[4]

So, even before the Trump Tower meeting, we find the following intelligence services in motion and attempting to concoct illicit dirt about Trump and Putin: British intelligence, Ukrainian intelligence, the DNI and the CIA in the United States, the FBI, and NATO's Strategic Communications Service and its U.S. offshoots. But wait, as they say in infomercial sales, that's not even close to all involved.

According to *Foreign Policy Magazine* and others, on July 11, 2017, a hacker going by the name of "Johnnie Walker" published a trove of emails from the private account of Lieutenant Robert J. Otto, who is tasked to a secretive unit in the U.S. State Department focused on Russia. *Newsweek* magazine states that Otto is the nation's "foremost" intelligence guy concerning Russia. The emails have not been authenticated. However, they include an email purported to have been written on the day of the Trump Tower meeting between Otto and Kyle Parker, of the House Committee on Foreign Affairs, featuring a picture of Russian attorney Natalia Velselnitskaya's house in Russia. Parker credits himself as the actual author of the Magnitsky Act sanctions against Russia, and a close friend of Bill Browder. Velselnitskaya claims that her children have been threatened as a result of her participation in a legal case questioning the bona fides of Bill Browder and the factual foundations of the Magnitsky Act. The picture of her house in this context suggests another level of intense surveillance directed at Trump Tower on the day of the meeting, and the possibility that threats to her family were actually governing Veselnitskaya's behavior.

The Set-Up

On June 3, Trump Jr. was emailed by publicist Ron Goldstone, a British national who operates out of the

nataliaveselnitskaya/facebook

Natalia Veselnitskaya

CC/Hudson Institute

British intelligence operative William Browder.

U.S., whose first career was as a British tabloid journalist. Goldstone's Facebook account appears to indicate that he is presently on a break from his businesses and on a world tour of gay bathhouses in which the proudly obese Goldstone takes pictures of himself wearing various strange hats and shirts in the company of young men. Who is financing this tour apparently outside the reach of Grand Jury subpoenas? Goldstone has also been photographed with Kathy Griffin, who famously posted a picture of herself with President Trump's severed head.

Goldstone emailed Donald Trump, Jr. that Aras Agalarov wanted Goldstone to set up a meeting with Trump, Jr. in which sensitive Russian government files about Hillary Clinton's dealings with Russia would be provided to the Trump campaign as a gesture of official Russian government support of the campaign. Trump Jr. agreed to the meeting.

Goldstone is the publicist for Emin Agalarov, an Azerbarjani pop star. Aras Agalarov and his son Emin partnered with Trump for the 2013 Miss Universe pageant in Moscow. The base of operations for the Agalarov family is the Moscow regional government, not Putin's Kremlin.

The actual twenty-minute meeting involved Russian attorney Natalia Veselnitskaya, who did most of the speaking by all accounts; Rinat Akhmetshin, a well-known Washington D.C.-based lobbyist and American citizen; Ike Kaveladze, a U.S. citizen and vice-presi-

---

4. The official British government file also probably included surveillance of apartments at Trump Tower associated with a then ongoing investigation of a Russian organized crime ring said to operate there and figures involved in the FIFA corruption investigation who also lived there. The FIFA investigation was worked by the FBI Eurasian Organized Crime Strike Force and Christopher Steele.

dent at one of the Agalarov's companies; Ron Goldstone; and the translator for Natalia Veselnitskaya, Anatoli Samochornov. Samochornov is also an American citizen who worked with Veselnitskaya frequently, since she does not speak English. He has also worked extensively for the FBI and the U.S. State Department. Although Akhmetshin has been linked to Russian counterintelligence repeatedly in the news media, that all appears to be based on his bragging about his two-year stint in the Russian military as a young man. The topic addressed by Veselnitskaya was the Magnitsky Act sanctions against Russia, which resulted from a campaign conducted by violently anti-Putin British operative William Browder, allied with Senator John McCain and the D.C. public relations firm Ashcroft and Glover.

Any sound investigation about this meeting would focus on who, out of the small army of intelligence operatives watching this meeting, designed and implemented the clear entrapment attempt against Donald Trump, Jr. for later use. Since it was surveilled and recorded by multiple intelligence agencies tripping all over one another at the time, (you get the image of Keystone cops), why was it only surfaced as the "smoking gun" recently?

Natalia Veselnitskaya had been paroled into the United States to serve as the Russian lawyer in a legal case in the Southern District of New York based solely on money-laundering allegations made by Bill Browder against her Russian clients. At the time of the Trump Tower meeting, however, Veselnitskaya was traveling on a business visa issued by the U.S. Department of State after having been previously denied such a visa, and after efforts by the U.S. Attorney for the Southern District of New York to prevent any free travel by her in the U.S. at all. Immigration attorneys I have spoken to describe this situation as extremely strange.

4. Obama's Final Days In Office—
Insurrection Against the President-Elect, Felonious Leaks

In an apparent effort to influence the Electoral College vote following the election, the Obama Administration leaked a preliminary intelligence community "assessment" that the Russians had hacked the Democrats' computers and otherwise intervened to swing the election to Donald Trump. According to the *New York Times* of March 1, 2017, Obama and his national security colleagues additionally spent the months after the election and prior to President Trump's inauguration dropping a trail of "leads" in official documents and leaking information, in the effort to delegitimize Trump and to continue their policies against Russia and China.

Certainly, there is a document trail on this process which appears to be confined to a period of a little over two months. Evelyn Farkas, formerly of the Defense Department's Russia, Ukraine, Eurasia Desk and the Atlantic Council, virtually admitted to MSNBC in March that she had participated in this process. This is where the illegal unmasking of names in FISA and E.O. 12333 surveillance occurred, when these crimes were committed. Samantha Power, the U.N. Ambassador, was reportedly involved in 260 unmasking requests bearing little relationship to her function. Other targets of the House Intelligence Committee concerning illegal unmasking and leaks include Susan Rice, John Brennan, and Ben Rhodes.

On Dec. 15, 2016, DNI James Clapper signed new procedures allowing the NSA to distribute raw intercept data throughout the entire intelligence community. These procedures became official on Jan. 3, 2017 when Attorney General Loretta Lynch signed off on them.

At issue is modification of secret procedures under E.O. 12333, deemed by Edward Snowden and others as the most significant authority for our present, completely unconstitutional surveillance state. Previously, the NSA was required to filter and redact information regarding U.S. citizens monitored in foreign counterintelligence activities. DNI Clapper had also implemented a cloud intelligence data platform accessible by all intelligence agencies, and obliterating many paper and digital access trails and safeguards. Were these new procedures implemented in any way based on a desire to facilitate leaks and obscure their origin to future investigators?

5. The January Blackmail/Extortion Attempt

On Jan. 6, 2017, according to James Comey's June 8th Congressional testimony, the intelligence chiefs went to Trump Tower to present the Obama Administration's report on Russian hacking, hoping to convince the skeptical President-elect to abandon his campaign promise for better relations with Putin and Russia. Following that briefing, in a pre-arranged move with the rest of Obama's intelligence directors, Comey cleared the room of everyone but himself and Trump. He presented Trump with the Steele dossier's most salacious allegations, namely that Trump had engaged in sexually perverse acts with Russian prostitutes while visiting

Moscow, and Putin had taped it. This is exactly what the infamous J. Edgar Hoover did—blackmail Washington politicians with FBI dossiers, assuring them that he could protect them so long as they did as Hoover wished. In fact, Comey described this as a "J. Edgar Hoover moment" in answers to questions by Senator Susan Collins on June 8. Dick Morris describes the entire affair as "just about as close as you can get to a political assassination without holding a gun to the President's head."

Senate Intelligence Committee

Left to right: former FBI director James Comey, former Director of National Intelligence James Clapper, and John Brennan, former head of the CIA.

Trump appears to have demanded that the entirely fake dossier be investigated, and refused to back down, in efforts to achieve better relations with Russia. In fact, Trump denounced the intelligence community publicly as acting like Nazis. He also denounced the McCarthyite hysteria they were generating. While Comey recorded the President-elect's responses on a classified computer moments after leaving him, Buzzfeed, which had frequently published raw Clinton/Obama "oppo" stories, published the December 2016 British/Clinton dodgy dossier in full. The U.S. intelligence community, particularly Obama's ghoulish grand inquisitor, CIA head John Brennan, proceeded to give it credibility by leaking that both President-elect Trump and President Obama had been briefed on its contents.

Publication of the Trump Russian sex allegations accompanied James Clapper's factless "official intelligence community assessment" that the Russians hacked the DNC and Podesta, and that they did so to influence the election in favor of Donald Trump. Put together by analysts hand-picked by the CIA's John Brennan, that assessment was backed by no actual evidence. It has now been thoroughly debunked as "the hack that wasn't" by the analysis presented by the Veteran's Intelligence Professionals for Sanity. John Brennan subsequently explained to Congress and the public that he does not "do evidence."

The Democrats, the news media, and their Republican allies led by John McCain and Lindsay Graham, went berserk over the factless Obama Administration "assessment," demanding special prosecutors and Congressional investigations, and sneering that "other shoes" were about to drop. The *New York Times'* Thomas Friedman, having clearly lost it, claimed that Russia had committed an "act of war," presumably seeking to invoke Article 5 of the NATO treaty.

6. The President Calls Out Comey, Brennan et al. for Wiretapping Him: They Lie About It To Congress

On March 4, 2017, after General Flynn was fired, and after a deluge of leaks of classified surveillance of members of Trump's transition and national defense teams, President Trump interrupted the entire fake media narrative by tweeting what had become obvious: that Obama had him "wiretapped" in Trump Tower prior to the election, and that what was happening to him reeked of McCarthyism. The media, which had been publishing allegations about FISA warrants and intercepts of Trump or his associates for months, erupted in what has to be one the most shameless demonstrations of the Big Lie ever known. They declared that Trump was offering wild claims with no evidence, essentially circling back on their very own reporting and labeling it, "fake news."

Now it has been revealed that FISA warrants existed on Paul Manafort from 2014 through some period in 2016, and from some period in 2016 through this year, conveniently omitting the period when he was Trump's campaign manager. Manafort lives in Trump Tower, and was originally investigated under the Foreign Agents Registration Act for his Ukraine activities. It is fairly obvious that the June 2016 meeting at Trump Tower was the subject of massive surveillance. It is also abundantly clear from the leaks which occurred concerning contacts with the Russians by Trump's campaign officials and supporters, that the Trump Tower offices of his transition were subject to massive surveillance, either as the result of extant FISA warrants or under E.O. 12333.

James Comey and James Clapper were both asked directly in their appearances before Congressional Committees whether there was any evidence at all to substantiate the President's wiretapping claims. Both of them gave emphatic answers that there was not, and went out of their respective ways to paint the President as a paranoid wacko.

So now, Robert Mueller is investigating the President of the United States for obstruction of justice, because he fired an FBI Director who lied to Congress. Really?

7. The Comey Firing-Attempted Entrapment of the President

On March 20, 2017, former FBI Director Comey breathed new life into what was, by then, an insurrection which had run out of steam. People were simply tired of Democrats, like Adam Schiff,[5] trying on McCarthyite tinfoil hats before TV cameras and pontificating about the outrage *du jour*. Comey, in testimony before the House Select Committee on Intelligence, made it officially public, for the first time, that the FBI had been investigating collusion between the Trump campaign and Russian interference in the election since July of 2016. He opined that the FBI counterintelligence investigation (which had been leaking like a sieve since its instigation in July, without producing any verifiable facts about either Russian interference or Trump campaign collusion) could continue for many more months, if not years. He refused to say whether the President himself was under investigation, despite the fact that he had told the President that he was not, and had told Congress the same thing behind closed doors.

Despite the daily press instructions about events which the public must view as scandalous (why scandalous was never explained), and highly publicized Congressional hearings concerning "Russia! Russia! Russia!" all of President Obama's men, at this late date, had only managed to arrange the human sacrifice of Michael Flynn for lying to the Vice-President about his conversations with the Russian ambassador in December.[6] They had also generated ethics, foreign intelligence registration, and tax questions about their other Trump campaign targets—typical of what happens when an entire life is put under a microscope, in a dedicated search for something, anything, that could be construed feasibly as wrongdoing.

Ask yourself, what have any of these people allegedly done? Spoken with the Russians? Talked about lifting sanctions imposed because Putin reacted to a coup Obama ran against the duly elected government of Ukraine? Lobbied on behalf of foreign governments? Really?

The actual testimony of Obama's intelligence officials before Congressional Committees, shorn of the media hype surrounding it, was that there was absolutely no evidence of any Trump campaign collusion with alleged Russian efforts to interfere in the U.S. elections. In fact, on March 15, 2017, Comey himself had told Senators Chuck Grassley and Diane Feinstein behind closed doors, that the President was not a target of his investigations, despite planted press stories to the contrary. Comey had otherwise continually stonewalled Grassley concerning the Senator's persistent questions about the FBI's relationship to British operative Christopher Steele.

While unable to produce any saleable legal goods, the illicit investigations had significantly bogged down the President's political agenda, while fostering an increasingly toxic and divisive national political environment. The strategy of official Washington, the Republicans who opposed the President's election, the Obama/Clinton Democratic establishment, and the intelligence

---

5. Schiff has a watermelon face combining features of the comic Charlie Brown and a Conehead; his personality is like the grasping and crazy personality of Peanuts cartoon character, Lucy Van Pelt. As a prosecutor it took him three tries to convict the hapless former FBI agent Richard Miller of espionage despite overwhelming and salacious evidence.

6. Flynn's scalping itself was the result of the unmasking of Flynn's name and illegal leaks of the same to the press as a result of classified surveillance. This fact was obliterated by sensational press coverage of the hyperventilated visit of Obama Assistant Attorney General Sally Yates to the White House to warn, nonsensically, that Flynn had been "compromised" by the Russians because he lied to the Vice-President. Exactly how this makes any sense at all we have not been told. Shakespeare's Macbeth intoned, "it is a tale, told by an idiot, full of sound and fury, signifying nothing."

agencies operating on behalf of British strategic policies and axioms is clear—use complicit Republicans to trap the President in failed and obnoxious policies, such as the healthcare bill; hope that the President's silent majority remains exactly that—silent; hope that some of the smelly stuff they are throwing up against the wall actually sticks; distract, distract, distract the President, and prevent him from working with Russia and China to develop the world, end wars, and implement the massive infrastructure and space exploration projects which will actually save our economy.

On May 3, 2017, Comey followed his March drama-queen performance before the House, with even more theatrical speechifying before the Senate Judiciary Committee. He bloviated that despite the fact that his unprecedented disclosures and handling of the Clinton email investigation may have impacted the election, and it made him nauseous, he, Mr. Eagle Scout and True Crime Detective rolled into one, would do the same thing all over again. He exaggerated the significance of the Anthony Weiner computer discovery by stating that it contained thousands of new Clinton emails, not previously produced, some of which were classified—a statement the FBI had to subsequently correct. As Assistant Attorney General Rod Rosenstein rightly argued, Comey violated numerous Justice Department regulations and ethical norms in his outrageous actions in the Clinton email investigation. It is the Attorney General's job to prosecute cases —to open and close them—not that of the FBI.

At the same Senate Judiciary hearing, Comey refused to state publicly that President Trump was not under investigation, despite repeatedly assuring the President of that fact privately. He knew this allowed the media and Democratic party "color revolution" to continue. He refused to confirm that there was any investigation into the torrent of illegal classified leaks at the center of the media campaign.

On May 9, President Trump fired Comey, setting the stage for Robert Mueller's appointment as Special Prosecutor. At the center of Mueller's inquiry will be a conspiracy to obstruct justice charge against the President for firing James Comey, along with any so-called process crimes he can find during his investigation—registration offenses under the Foreign Agents Registration Act, tax offenses, or false statements to FBI agents or Congress. As he builds his case, Mueller will follow his standard playbook, putting unrelenting psychological pressure on those Trump loyalists he can implicate in the process crimes. He will continue to target and investigate the President's family for similar offenses in order to destabilize the President himself. He will continue the relentless demonization of the President, in order to ensure that neutral officials in Washington who witnessed key events will testify not according to the truth, but according to what they see as future career prospects.

Following his firing, Comey and friends leaked to the press notes which he had allegedly taken following most of his encounters with the President. With each encounter, Comey's leaked account says, he returned to discuss what was said and its implications with a close circle of his FBI comrades. He prepared for each encounter with the President based on "murder boards" conducted by his FBI colleagues. In the course of their meetings, Comey says, the President asked for his loyalty, which Comey portrayed like the request of some mafia don in a bad Hollywood movie. If it happened, such a request, in the context of what appeared to be an open insurrection against the President by the intelligence community, is hardly surprising. The President denies that it happened.

On the day after the President fired Flynn, according to Comey, the President cleared the room and went one on one with him, expressing the "hope" that Comey could let the matter of Michael Flynn go. Comey whines that he took the President's "hope" as an "order," giving rise to concerns about possible obstruction of justice. This line of reasoning was thoroughly eviscerated by Senator James Risch in the Senate Judicary Committee hearing on June 8, 2017. Senator Risch forced Comey to admit that Trump never ordered him to let the Flynn matter go, but only expressed a "hope" that he would do so, and no prosecution that Comey knew of ever went forward, based on someone expressing "hope" for something. While the President denies he ever asked Comey to let the Flynn matter go, Harvard Law Professor Emeritus and famed trial lawyer Alan Dershowitz writes that the President would be fully within his legal and constitutional prerogatives to order Comey to back off Flynn. He could have simply told Comey, I am going to pardon Flynn.

So, it is clear by James Comey's own account that he was trying to set the President up, to entrap him—an escapade which was "crudely" interrupted when the President fired him. Again, confirming this, Comey told Senator Susan Collins in his testimony, that the reason why he did not stop the President from improper inter-

Former FBI director James Comey (left), and prosecutor Robert Mueller (right).

actions, if he thought they were such, the reason he concealed the alleged improper and possibly illegal conduct from his superiors at the Justice Department, and the reason he did not resign, was because his encounters with the President were of "investigative interest" to the FBI. Otherwise, Comey's leaks reveal a man so leery of even shaking the President's hand (or being photographed doing it) that once in January he tried to hide himself in the White House drapes in the hopes that Trump would not see him.

The problem for Robert Mueller's obstruction case, among others, is that both Comey and his Assistant Andrew McCabe have previously testified, under oath, to Congress that there was no pressure to end the FBI's investigations from anyone in the Trump Administration. And, Comey confirmed in his testimony that prior to his firing, Trump was not under investigation for collusion with Russia, obstruction, or any other offense. Further, Comey has proved that he is willing to violate professional norms and Justice Department regulations, if not laws, by leaking government documents. The question is, what else was leaked by Comey and his FBI circle? Finally, we now know that Comey lied to or misled Congress about the "wiretaps" on Trump Tower—the Manafort FISA warrants prove the case. Senator Grassley has asked the FBI: Why, if you were wiretapping a close associate of the President, wouldn't you warn the President about him as is customarily done? The true answer is that the President himself was and is the target of an unprecedented and illegal coup-attempt conducted by those sworn to uphold the Constitution and the nation's laws.

Those familiar with the relationship between Comey and Robert Mueller describe them as "joined at the hip," "cut from the same cloth" (can't help thinking of the Union Jack), close personal friends, and mentor (Mueller) to mentee (Comey). The problem with this relationship is that Department of Justice conflict guidelines specifically bar prosecutors (Mueller) from investigating issues where close friends (Comey) have a significant role, such as material witnesses. Official Washington knows all of this and yet touts this investigation as somehow "independent," "apolitical," and "unconflicted."

Will You Help Us End This Coup?

So, now you know. Since the election and before, we have been stuck in a very elaborate and dangerous British hoax, gambling the future of our nation in a cold coup against an elected president. Actual crimes have been committed—not by the President—but against the President and the Constitution. What has happened is that political differences, ideas, have been criminalized, the very danger most provisions of our Constitution and its Bill of Rights were explicitly designed to guard against.

We have shown you the prosecutorial robot named Robert Mueller, whom others have always pointed to shoot, and why he has been deployed to take out the President of the United States. We have told you the real reasons why the President has been attacked by a foreign power, the British and their allies in our country. We have shown you that many of the same people and methods were deployed on a smaller scale to deprive the world of the beautiful ideas of Lyndon LaRouche. Now, at a point where this President, freed of Mueller and adequately advised, could join with China's Belt and Road and usher in a new renaissance for mankind, shouldn't we really, finally, win our future, this time?

'To Soar, Refuse To Creep or Crawl': Remembering W. Allen Salisbury

by Dennis Speed

Sept. 25—The LaRouche *Four Laws*:

- re-implementation of Glass-Steagall,
- simultaneous immediate issuance of emergency credit earmarked exclusively for improvements in the nation's physical-economic productive capability,
- a reorganized national credit system, and
- an international "science-driver" creating a new "extra-terrestrial" economic platform based on thermonuclear fusion power applications,

is a singular development in human history. If implemented, the world would experience the highest rates of human growth in what LaRouche calls "potential relative population density" in the history of the planet—with less crowding, pollution, war, famine, and disease than at any prior time. There is no alternative to these Four Laws. That, however, does not mean that humanity will adopt this course of action.

Two score years ago, a great American, a friend of Lyndon LaRouche, attempted "to hold the mirror up to nature, to show virtue her own feature" by revealing to the United States of the late 1970s and 1980s, the proud tradition of American economists and statesmen that had been forgotten by their countrymen. He and LaRouche were not listened to. In 1989, LaRouche and several associates were imprisoned. In September 1992, a quarter century ago, Allen Salisbury (1949-1992) died of cancer at the age of 43. It is with the intention to prevent the repeat of that tragic refusal of Americans to listen then, and the catastrophic consequences which followed, that this remembrance of Salisbury's collaboration with LaRouche is offered. Now, at this time, it were appropriate to retrieve his fighting standard for the immediate battle to win the fight to have the Presidency adopt the LaRouche Four Laws without delay.

Allen Salisbury
(1949-1992)

W. Allen Salisbury, author of the groundbreaking 1978 book, *The Civil War and the American System: America's Battle with Britain, 1860-1876*, would have laughed uproariously at the present seeming paradox of American politics. He would have found it poetic justice that it would be a President Donald Trump—a figure formerly very familiar to Salisbury, and to those who were "in the streets of New York" in 1977—who would be the first American President since William McKinley to refer to "the American System" in speeches in Michigan and Kentucky only shortly after taking the oath of President in January of this year. This would have struck Salisbury as especially fitting, after the Obama Administration's eight year "malign neglect" of the "lower 80%" of Americans, and the all-out assault by Obama against the scientific optimism of the Kennedy-era space program, as advanced in the 1987 LaRouche-Salisbury video essay, "*The Woman On Mars*." In that video, LaRouche says:

"In a nationwide TV broadcast a few weeks ago

["Who Is Lyndon LaRouche?" Feb. 4, 1988], I told you that on my first day as President I shall declare a national economic emergency, and launch the largest economic recovery program in our history. During each of the first two years of my administration, about $2 trillions in low-cost federal loans will be invested in building up our nation's presently rotting industrial infrastructure plus building up about five million new industrial jobs during the first three or four years of my administration. Looking back to the experience of the 1940-1943 period under President Franklin Roosevelt, we know that the recovery will creak at the beginning, but will build up speed over the first two years, so that by about the third year the United States will have the highest per capita income in our history.

"There are no mysterious tricks involved; it is all basic economics modeled upon our successful economic recoveries under Franklin Roosevelt and John F. Kennedy. However, to keep that recovery going, beyond the first three to four years, and to make our economy once again the most competitive on Earth, we must invest in creating new technologies. To do that, we must pick up where we left off with the old Apollo program, back during the 1960s. The old aerospace program of the 1960s paid back more than ten cents for every penny we invested in it. This Mars program will pay us back much, much more—not 40 years from now, but each year over the 50 years or more to come. This project's spinoffs, in the form of new products and new technologies into our civilian economy, mean that, by the year 2027 A.D., the average person in the United States will have a real income at least ten times that of today.

"As you know, my specialty is a branch of

EIRNS/Philip Ulanowsky

Allen Salisbury in consultation with Lyndon LaRouche, during the taping of a television show, Boston, 1988.

physical economy founded by Leibniz, called physical economy. Over the years, my associates and I have had the privilege of working with some of the world's leading scientists in plasma physics, optical biophysics, and space technology. What I have done, is to put this scientific knowledge together with my own expertise in physical economy, just as I did back in 1982 when I proposed what became known as the SDI...."

Salisbury's job was to take this conception of LaRouche, the most advanced form of economic thought, not only in American but world history, and assist LaRouche in visualizing that for an American audience. This gave Salisbury, in turn, a way to implicitly restate his own, earlier historical researches on what has been termed "the American System" from a far more advanced standpoint.

How Salisbury Rediscovered and Helped Redefine the American System

There are several persons that used the term "American System," and used it differently, during the Nineteenth Century. What Salisbury's book did was to acquaint his readers with the deeper, "Leibnizian" principle of progress behind the idea, and particularly Abraham Lincoln's idea, of the American System as best expressed in the person and Presidency of Abraham Lincoln. (Lincoln's 1860 campaign speech, "Discoveries and Inventions," beginning with the sentence, "All creation is a mine, and every man a miner," expounded this principle, sometimes termed "the machine-tool principle," as the core of his anti-slavery doctrine.) Discoveries and inventions that decrease the need for human "muscle power" and increase the use and need for human cognition, when applied to the physical transformation of nature, are the basis for society to evolve a "more perfect union" of the idea of the sovereign nation state with the Idea of Progress.

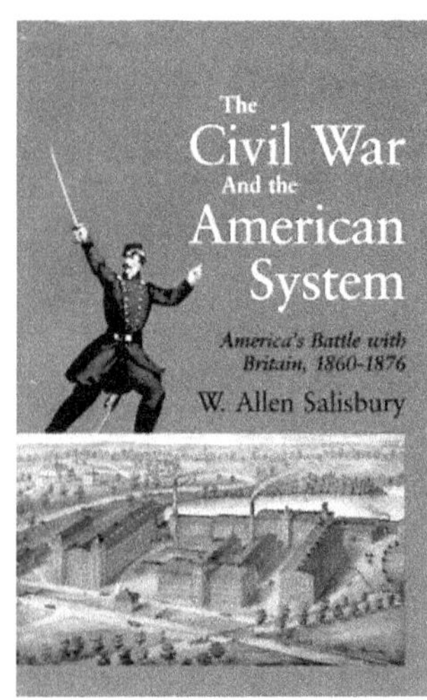

Cover of Allen Salisbury's book. Salisbury rediscovered that the core of Abraham Lincoln's opposition to slavery was the Leibnizian principle of progress.

In that idea, slavery is recognized for what it was—not the basis for the building of the United States, but the basis for the holding back of progress in the United States. That is what Abraham Lincoln opposed. The opponent was not only black chattel slavery in America. The United States was opposed to slavery everywhere on the planet. Lincoln's alliance with Czar Alexander II, as mediated through the great Cassius Marcellus Clay of Kentucky, Lincoln's ambassador to Russia, was explicitly against the slave power of Britain. Russian fleet deployments to New York and San Francisco in 1862 were the same thing. Russian land negotiations such as the American purchase of Alaska, with the Lincoln Administration's William Seward, were conducted precisely to the purpose of strengthening the continental power of the United States and destroying the maritime power of the British navy and British commerce.

Slavery had been continuously imposed by the British banking interests on the United States, from the Sixteenth Century through the time of Lincoln. It was Lincoln's transcontinental war with the British slave power, which was mistakenly called the "Civil War." This is why Salisbury referred to a sixteen-year conflict with the British, not a four-year conflict "between the North and the South." And this is why the British assassinated Abraham Lincoln—both for what Lincoln had done, but even more, for what he was about to do. Though Lincoln would not live to realize his intention of Reconstruction, he nevertheless succeeded in deploying

the Constitutional intent of Alexander Hamilton's Presidential design of the U.S. Treasury to create the most productive economy in world history while at the same time fighting and winning America's most physically self-destructive war.

The United States experienced a net loss in physical wealth through slavery. It was the faction of physical economists out of Philadelphia, centered around Matthew Carey, his son Henry Carey, and their friend, the German economist Friedrich List, that were the champions of the American System Philadelphia school. Carey's 1853 work, *The Slave Trade, Domestic And Foreign, Why It Exists And How It May Be Extinguished* is still one of the most thorough, and thoroughly unread refutations of slavery ever written. Carey assaulted slavery not merely in the United States, but Ireland, Portugal, Turkey, Scotland, and India, as well.

List's emphasis on the development of railroads in Pennsylvania, combined with the successful completion of the Erie Canal in 1825, was reconceptualized by Lincoln's "Carey faction" as the Transcontinental Railroad which Lincoln commissioned almost as soon as he walked in the door of the White House. That transcontinental Railway system is the primary poetic metaphor that is now being realized through what is termed the World Land-Bridge proposed by Helga and Lyndon LaRouche as a next-generation "New Silk Road," which the present Trump Administration should adopt as American policy in the image of Abraham Lincoln's war against the British. Given that it is the British that have already sought to "impeach or remove by other methods" the American President, through illegal and treasonous means, the present administration should leap at the chance to thus finally correct the wrong done by the 1865 assassination of Abraham Lincoln.

The Poetic Method in Science and Strategy

The detective work through which Salisbury was led to unearth the thoroughly buried-in-plain-sight Henry Carey was once characterized by him as "How to Smell a Rat While Reading History Books." Simultaneous with his work on the War of Britain's Confederacy Against the Union, Salisbury was beginning the reha-

Friedrich List

Henry Carey

Mathew Carey

bilitation of poet Edgar Poe (Edgar "Allan" Poe), one of the most important minds produced in America. Poe, a precocious military intelligence officer trained at West Point, was a lifelong, savage opponent of British Romanticism, and used his various stories, essays, and literary criticism to skewer the British and their American apologists, very much as Jonathan Swift had done one hundred years earlier. Poe's powerful insight into the post-Revolutionary War "battle for the mind" taking place in America was best expressed in his invention of the detective story. He invented the form, creating the character C. August Dupin, but also solving real crimes as he did in the case of Mary Rogers of New York City ("The Mystery of Marie Roget"). Salisbury applied his understanding of Poe's method in his work as an historian, organizer, and film-maker.

Salisbury knew, as Lyndon LaRouche once said, commenting on the works of Poe, that "poetry must supersede mathematics in physics." LaRouche collaborated with Salisbury on the production of several of the former's Presidential television broadcasts. Particularly notable was their joint work on 1987's groundbreaking "The Woman On Mars." The use of the musical tones and intervals derived from Kepler's Platonic hypothesis of the solar system, juxtaposed with the opening of Mozart's C Major "Dissonance" quartet, expressed the congruence of human creativity and the laws of the "non-human" universe. The "curvature" underlying the astrophysical, biophysical, microphysical, and human creative expressions of a single universal nature was given wing using the metaphor of human space flight. This was Salisbury's way of illustrating the idea behind Poe's famous passage from his 1848 *Eureka: A Prose Poem*, in which Poe was referring to a mythical person:

"Yes, Kepler was essentially a theorist; but this title, now of so much sanctity, was, in those ancient days, a designation of supreme contempt. It is only now that men begin to appreciate that divine old man—to sympathize with the prophetical and poetical rhapsody of his ever-memorable words. For my part," continues the unknown correspondent, "I glow with a sacred fire when I even think of them, and feel that I shall never grow weary of their repetition:—in concluding this letter, let me have the real pleasure of transcribing them once again:—'I care not whether my work be read now or by posterity. I can afford to wait a century for readers when God himself has waited six thousand years for an observer. I triumph. I have stolen the golden secret of the Egyptians. I will indulge my sacred fury.'

This is not the voice of Poe, but "from a somewhat remarkable letter, which appears to have been found corked in a bottle and floating on the Mare Tenebrarum—an ocean well described by the Nubian geographer, Ptolemy Hephestion, but little frequented in modern days.... The date of this letter, I confess, surprises me even more particularly than its contents; for it seems to have been written in the year Two thousand eight hundred and forty-eight. As for the passages I am about to transcribe, they, I fancy, will speak for themselves."

Poe, in the "Irritating" ironical-polemical style

characteristic of the best of writers and thinkers, described the inside of British thinking, which has now become nearly universal among Americans, in this age of the Internet and the "Google word-search."

"Do you know, my dear friend," says the writer, addressing, no doubt, a contemporary—"Do you know that it is scarcely more than eight or nine hundred years ago since the metaphysicians first consented to relieve the people of the singular fancy that there exist but two practicable roads to Truth? Believe it if you can! It appears, however, that long, long ago, in the night of Time, there lived a Turkish philosopher called Aries and surnamed Tottle." [Here, possibly, the letter-writer means Aristotle; the best names are wretchedly corrupted in two or three thousand years.] "The fame of this great man depended mainly upon his demonstration that sneezing is a natural provision, by means of which over-profound thinkers are enabled to expel superfluous ideas through the nose; but he obtained a scarcely less valuable celebrity as the founder, or at all events as the principal propagator, of what was termed the deductive or *a priori* philosophy. He started with what he maintained to be axioms, or self-evident truths:—and the now well-understood fact that no truths are self-evident, really does not make in the slightest degree against his speculations:—it was sufficient for his purpose that the truths in question were evident at all. From axioms he proceeded, logically, to results. His most illustrious disciples were one Tuclid, a geometrician," [meaning Euclid] "and one Kant, a Dutchman, the originator of that species of Transcendentalism which, with the change merely of a C for a K, now bears his peculiar name.

"Well, Aries Tottle flourished supreme, until the advent of one Hog, surnamed 'the Ettrick shepherd,' who preached an entirely different system, which he called the *a posteriori* or in-

Allen Salisbury displays a gift presented to him during a 1979 lecture tour.

ductive. His plan referred altogether to sensation. He proceeded by observing, analyzing, and classifying facts—instantiae Naturae, as they were somewhat affectedly called—and arranging them into general laws. In a word, while the mode of Aries rested on noumena, that of Hog depended on phenomena; and so great was the admiration excited by this latter system that, at its first introduction, Aries fell into general disrepute.

"Finally, however, he recovered ground, and was permitted to divide the empire of Philosophy with his more modern rival:—the savans contenting themselves with proscribing all other competitors, past, present, and to come; putting an end to all controversy on the topic by the promulgation of a Median law, to the effect that the Aristotelian and Baconian roads are, and of right ought to be, the sole possible avenues to knowledge:—'Baconian,' you must know, my dear friend," adds the letter-writer at this point, "was an adjective invented as equivalent to Hog-ian, and at the same time more dignified and euphonious.

"Now I do assure you most positively"—proceeds the epistle—"that I represent these matters fairly; and you can easily understand how restrictions so absurd on their very face must have operated, in those days, to retard the progress of true Science, which makes its most important advances—as all History will show—by seemingly intuitive leaps. These ancient ideas confined investigation to crawling; and I need not suggest to you that crawling, among varieties of locomotion, is a very capital thing of its kind;— but because the tortoise is sure of foot, for this reason must we clip the wings of the eagles? For many centuries, so great was the infatuation, about Hog especially, that a virtual stop was put to all thinking, properly so called. No man dared utter a truth for which he felt himself indebted to his soul alone. It mattered not whether the truth was even demonstrably such; for the dogmatizing philosophers of that epoch regarded only the road by which it professed to have been attained. The end, with them, was a point of no moment, whatever:—'the means!' they vociferated—'let us look at the means!'—and if, on scrutiny of the means, it was found to come neither under the category Hog, nor under the category Aries (which means ram), why then the savans went no farther, but, calling the thinker a fool and branding him a 'theorist,' would never, thenceforward, have any thing to do either with him or with his truths."

In a Preface released shortly after Salisbury's death in September 1992 at the age of 43, his wife Pat observed, "Allen wielded the method of metaphor and humor to address the universal in his reader, whatever the topic. As Poe wrote, Allen's "harshest idea will to melody run."

Salisbury's interest was not in the mythical Edgar Poe, mistakenly known as "Edgar Allen Poe," a name which Poe himself rarely used and would have detested. It was, rather in the Poe that was a member of the extended secret intelligence service that had been established by Washington, Hamilton, Lafayette, and others as the Society of Cincinnatus. In his article, "Edgar Allan Poe: The Lost Soul of America," Salisbury tells us:

"That Poe planned to go to France to aid the allies of Lafayette is clear in this letter that he wrote to Commandant Thayer of West Point shortly after his departure from the Academy:

'Sir: Having no longer any ties which can bind me to my native country, I intend by the first opportunity to proceed to Paris with the view of obtaining through the interest of the Marquis de Lafayette, an appointment (if possible) in the Polish Army. In the event of the interference of France in behalf of Poland this may easily be effected—at all events it will be my only feasible plan of procedure.

"'The object of this letter is respectfully to re-

The Marqis de Lafayette in New York in 1825, at the end of his tour of all 24 American states in support of John Quincy Adams' Presidential campaign.

quest that you will give me such assistance as may lie in your power in the furtherance of my views.

"'A certificate of standing in my class is all that I have any right to expect. Anything further— a letter to a friend in Paris—or to the Marquis— would be a kindness which I should never forget.'"

The name C. Auguste Dupin has also been the subject of much debate among Poe scholars. I will not bother here with some of the suggested sources for the name Dupin, since Poe could have been referring to one person only: Charles A. Dupin of Paris, a leading figure in the Ecole Polytechnique circles of Gaspard Monge, Lazard Carnot, and their associates. It is the Ecole Polytechnique method of scientific investigation that is the subject of Poe's detective tales, or 'tales of ratiocination,' as Poe more properly termed them.

This is no matter of mere conjecture or guesswork. Poe very early in life came under the influence of Supreme Court Justice John Marshall and General Winfield Scott in his home in Richmond, Virginia. In his early teens, Poe was selected to serve as second in command of the Richmond Junior Volunteers honor guard that accompanied Lafayette during his 1824 visit to the city. Lafayette's visit to Richmond, part of a months-long tour of the United States, was organized by the Cincinnatus Society to secure the Presidential election of John Quincy Adams and to raise funds for Lafayette's forces in Europe. As Salisbury stated:

> Marshall had been influential in helping to establish the Society of Cincinnatus, and Winfield Scott later became an honorary member of the society, with specific charge over matters of military intelligence. General Scott, together with Commandant Thayer, made several trips to Paris for the specific purpose of acquiring the necessary textbooks and related materials to firmly establish the tradition of the Ecole Polytechnique at West Point.

John Marshall

Gen. Winfield Scott

Unfortunately, Salisbury's death did not allow him to complete a book upon which he was working, tentatively entitled "Edgar Poe and the Whig CIA," which would have shed light on, in particular, the role of the Hudson River school of artists, writers, and poets at work on both sides of the divide for and against the legacy of the American Revolution.

In recent weeks, the importance of "the methods of investigation to determine the truth" has come more and more to the fore. The Russia-gate hoax has in particular provoked that discussion. In one extended exchange, the subject of Poe's methods of inquiry was raised. During that discussion, William Binney, the thirty-year NSA veteran who invented the ThinThread meta-data surveillance system, confessed to a great interest in the work of Edgar Poe. He is not yet familiar with the work of Allen Salisbury. It will be important for him, and for all Americans that want to learn "how to know the truth," to become more greatly acquainted with what he did, which can be done by reading writings of his made available through this publication. For now, we will indicate the domain of thought frequented by Salisbury in the words of his teacher and friend, LaRouche, as stated in LaRouche's essay, "A Non-Mystical View of the Necessity of Existence of the Notion of 'Absolute Time':

> "We have shown, as in earlier locations, that the space-time curvature of the creative processes is identical with that of astrophysical, microphysical, and biophysical space-time. This congruence is the sole basis for the possibility of real human knowledge of the universe. Thus, nothing called human knowledge is knowledge in fact, unless it expresses directly the product of creative-mental processes, as opposed to, for example, the axiomatic linearity of all formal deductive reasoning. Thus, only the intelligible representation of those mental acts of our species by which valid fundamental discoveries in physical science are generated, efficiently represents something truly appropriate to the connotations of 'scientific knowledge.'

> "The proof of this specific congruence permits and compels us to exercises of a form usefully termed 'very strong hypothesis,' in the same sense, approximately, that Leonardo da Vinci argued for his principle of hypothesis. The highest form of such activity is associated with the manifest possibility of our willful consciousness of the creative mental processes themselves. Once we have defined the requirements of intelligible representation of such creative-mental process, that intelligibility, made conscious, becomes an object of conscious thought for us. We are able to perform conscious operations, such as strong hypothesis, upon the processes of creative thought themselves.

> "In this way, we are obliged to address a set of higher-order questions respecting the lawful composition of our universe."

AUGUST 16, 1996

U.S. Law: Neither Truth Nor Justice

by Lyndon H. LaRouche, Jr.

The following statement was issued by the LaRouche Exploratory Committee on Aug. 16, 1996.

To the degree that U.S. Supreme Court's influential Associate Justice Antonin Scalia typifies the problem, there is no spirit of love for truth, or for justice, controlling the practice of law, in the U.S.A. today.

Typical, is the fact that an innocent man, political prisoner Michael Billington, still remains condemned to a 77-year, Virginia sentence, even after the evidence presented in several appeals has demonstrated the wrongfulness of his trial and sentence, and has also exposed the corrupt, political motives of both the prosecution and erring judges. In four, related cases, other innocent, political prisoners suffer comparably monstrous, if somewhat lesser terms. The widespread notoriety of the wrongs in these cases, calls attention to the flagrant quality of the rampant corruption within the U.S. justice system.[1] Typical, are U.S. Supreme Court majority decisions, expediting death-sentences, even in cases where compelling evidence of wrongful conviction was awaiting its proper hearing.[2] At best, even where

---

1. Billington was falsely tried, and convicted on charges arising from alleged sale of securities. Later impeachment, of the prosecution's perjured witnesses, demonstrated that there were no securities; therefore, had he been fairly tried, he would have been exonerated. At trial, through aid of a corrupted defense attorney and complicity of the trial judge, Billington was denied the opportunity to present the evidence which would have impeached the perjured prosecution witnesses. The indictment, trial, and appeals process, have been controlled, to date, by plainly manifest, most blatant, politically motivated judicial corruption, in both the Commonwealth and Federal courts.

2. *Herrera v. Collins,* for example. Leonel Herrera was executed on

A Ku Klux Klan rally. "The present form of the problem which Scalia's argument typifies," writes LaRouche, "dates to that specific degeneration of the Federal justice system, the which came to the surface when Ku Klux Klan Kleagle Hugo Black covered his white Klan robes with the black robes of a Supreme Court Justice."

corrupt political motives do not govern both the prosecution and the bench, the pathetic tradition of François Rabelais's fictional judges, Suckfist and Kissbreech, casting dice in the back room, to select the verdict, is widespread.

Insight into the problem is gained by reviewing this writer's own Federal case, tried in late 1988, in the Alexandria Federal District Court for the Eastern District of Virginia. Michael Billington was also among the co-defendants in that case.[3]

The 'LaRouche Case'

The *Federal prosecutors* in that case are on the record, as arguing, in 1987, that no successful prosecution of this writer, on "loan fraud" charges, could be made, as long as the relevant three political publishing firms, headquartered in Virginia, continued to make payments to their lenders. The prosecutors argued, that only if the Federal government acted to bankrupt the firms, and close them down, could Lyndon LaRouche be successfully charged.[4] After receiving the prosecutor's advice to this effect, the U.S. Department of Justice proceeded, unlawfully, with an unprecedented, and involuntary bankruptcy action against the three firms. The bankruptcy was used to close the firms down, and to cease the loan-repayments. This bankruptcy was judged, in 1989, after the three firms had been rendered defunct by the government, to have been unlawful; the courts found, that the U.S. Attorney, the same Henry Hudson directing the Alexandria Federal criminal case, "The 1988 LaRouche case," had accomplished his unlawful, 1987 bankrupting of the firms through aid of "objective fraud upon the court."[5]

When these same Federal prosecutors brought an indictment of this writer, Billington, et al., on Oct. 14, 1988, all of the charges included therein were subsumed under the single, principal charge of "conspiracy to commit loan fraud."[6] All of the charges in that case were based upon outstanding political loans to the three relevant publishing houses.

A crucial added feature of that Alexandria trial, in addition to the fraudulent charges themselves, was the role of a shamelessly corrupt trial judge, Albert V. Bryan, Jr. Thus, that Alexandria case is exemplary of the pervasive political corruption of today's U.S. Justice system: a case in which the combination, of a crooked Justice Department, and a politically corrupt judge, colluded in crafting a fraudulent prosecution.

Judge Bryan had figured significantly in furthering the political aims of the government's unlawful bankrupting of the three relevant firms. During mid-1987, Bryan rendered the decision which virtually assured the permanent closing of the three targetted publishing firms, thus ensuring that non-payment of loans which became the charge in the 1988 trial of Billington, et al. Bryan's decision contributed substantially to the irreparable harm suffered by the firms and their lenders,[7] harm caused by the unlawful involuntary bankruptcy action of the same, corrupt U.S. Attorney, Henry Hudson, who brought the 1988 "loan-fraud" case.[8]

The most significant among the numerous corrupt decisions rendered by Bryan in the 1988 Federal trial, was his Rule 403 *in limine* ruling, excluding from the trial all relevant evidence pertaining to both the Federal government's sole responsibility for the bankruptcy,

---

May 12, 1993 after the Supreme Court refused to hear new evidence of his innocence.

3. Case No. CR 88-243-A, *United States v. Lyndon H. LaRouche, Jr., William Wertz, Edward Spannaus, Michael Billington, Dennis Small, Paul Greenberg, Joyce Rubinstein*. See *Railroad! U.S.A. vs. Lyndon La-Rouche, et al.* (Washington, D.C.: Commission to Investigate Human Rights Violations, 1989). See also the report of an independent commission of international legal experts, released on Sept. 3, 1994, and published in *EIR*, Sept. 16, 1994, p. 43. Further information is provided in *Independent Hearings to Investigate Misconduct by the U.S. Department of Justice* (Washington, D.C.: Schiller Institute, October 1995).

4. "Motion to Vacate, Set Aside, Correct Sentence Under 28 USC §2255, *United States v. Lyndon LaRouche, case CA-92-86-AM, E.D. Va.," Exhibit 15.*

5. *In re Caucus Distributors, Inc. et al.,* 106 BR 890 (Bankruptcy E.D. Va. 1989), 907, 909, 926. Affirmed by U.S. District Judge Claude Hilton. The U.S. Solicitor General declined to appeal further.

6. All of the seven defendants were charged under the first count, of "conspiracy to commit loan fraud." Under that single count of conspiracy to commit loan-fraud, there were an additional, variously distributed, eleven "substantive counts," aggregating to an alleged $294,000 for all defendants combined, and an additional, subsidiary count, the esoteric ("Klein Conspiracy") charge of "attempt to impede and obstruct the functions of the Internal Revenue Service," on which only the present writer was charged. When sundry motions for severance of the "IRS" count were made, the prosecution insisted that the latter count was efficiently integral to the first count.

7. Although these loans were not given for electoral campaign activities, they were analogous to campaign loans in other respects. All of the relevant outstanding loans of the three publishing firms were of the "soft," political variety, which often carried no interest charges, and whose payment dates were not infrequently postponed by agreement with the lender. Thus, once Judge Bryan had made his mid-1987 decisions in the bankruptcy case, he virtually assured the defrauding of both the three firms, and non-payment of all loans outstanding as of the date of the Justice Department's unlawful bankruptcy of April 21, 1987.

8. This was the same Henry Hudson, who, as head of the U.S. Marshals Service, figured prominently in the U.S. Government's wrong-doing in the celebrated Weaver case.

and also his own role in preventing continued loan-re-payments. Otherwise, Judge Bryan's lack of moral character, was exhibited most luridly in his response to a *habeas corpus* in the same case, in which, to make short of the matter, he "lied his head off," on a highly relevant issue of the case.[9]

The prosecution in that case, and in the subsequent, fraudulent prosecution of Billington by the Commonwealth of Virginia, and so on, had its officially documented, political genesis in 1982-1983 actions by former Secretary of State Henry A. Kissinger, and actions taken by a faction of Kissinger's cronies inside the Reagan administration, launching a covert, politically motivated national security operation against this writer and his associates. Kissinger's cronies within the U.S. Justice Department's Criminal Division,[10] and in the apparatus of mob-linked Roy M. Cohn, et al., played a central role in this operation, over the interval beginning January 1983, and continuing through all of the notable cases of presently continuing mass-media and legal operations against the writer and his friends. All, or nearly all of the official and correlated record of the 1982-1988 phases of this continuing operation, and related governmental political corruption, were indicated to Judge Bryan, and available to him and all relevant Federal courts, at all relevant times, in these cases.[11]

If one includes the existing record for all the national, and international, covert operations conducted by the Kissinger State Department, the FBI, and others, against this writer and his associates, since 1968, including one officially documented, 1973, plot by the FBI, to arrange this writer's "elimination" by the Communist Party U.S.A., the crucial significance of the so-called "LaRouche" case is, in the words of former U.S. Attorney General Ramsey Clark, that it is the "most pervasive" of the instances of such governmental wrong-doing on record.[12]

The outstanding national and international significance of the Justice Department's corruption in the so-called "LaRouche cases," is better understood by showing the connection to the frauds of the same U.S. Justice Department in both the fraudulent activities of the Office of Special Investigation (OSI), and in racially motivated persecution of the class of elected African-American officials of Federal and state governments. Notable among the OSI cases, are the case of Cleveland auto-worker John Demjanjuk, and the less known, but related case of the assassinated Tscherim Soobzokov.

In both the Demjanjuk and Soobzokov cases, as in the LaRouche cases, the OSI's 1978-1979 targetting of its intended victims, was coordinated with the office of Rep. Elizabeth Holtzman (D-N.Y.). She was a principal co-sponsor of a bill establishing an arrangement piloted, earlier, by Secretary of State Henry A. Kissinger.

---

9. During the sentencing hearing in the 1988 case, in response to the statement of defendant Edward Spannaus, Bryan declared: "While counsel in the case haven't borne down on it, the defendants have repeatedly and from some of the testimony, raised this idea that this is a politically inspired, politically motivated prosecution. I reject that as arrant nonsense. The idea that this organization is a sufficient threat to anything, that would warrant the Government bringing a prosecution to silence them, just defies human experience." (Cited in *Railroad!* op. cit., p. 515-516. In pre-trial proceedings, Bryan had reviewed several, extensively documented motions showing cumulative attacks upon defendant LaRouche by leading news media, by both U.S.A. and foreign publications. He had ruled against allowing that relevant evidence in trial, and had also excluded, similar, massive documentation, from the Federal court record, and elsewhere, of relevant political operations run against LaRouche et al. by both governmental and accomplice agencies. In trial, Bryan had heard testimony on the importance of LaRouche's 1982-1984 activities with the Reagan Administration's National Security Council, and also relevant testimony from high-ranking officials of foreign nations. Either Judge Bryan was mentally impaired, or he was lying flagrantly, and his lying was, by its nature, politically motivated.
10. Deputy Assistant Attorneys-General John "Jack" Keeney and Mark Richard, et al.
11. As the fruit of a foreign-intelligence operation launched, in January 1983, at the prompting of Henry A. Kissinger, no part of the combined U.S. Federal, state, and foreign operations against LaRouche et al. were conducted within the confines of the customary pretenses of legality. Included were some of the same elements deployed against the later

defendants since January 1974, when the *New York Times* deployed to cover up the FBI's role in what an official FBI document, subsequently released under FOIA, confirms to have been a planned "elimination" of LaRouche. Shortly after the January action of Kissinger cronies leading into the October 1988 Alexandria indictment, beginning no later than April 1983, a multi-agency public-private task-force was created, featuring New York private banker, and Jimmy Goldsmith-family crony, John Train. Included in the case, from then through 1989, were the Anti-Defamation League (ADL), the *Wall Street Journal*, NBC-TV News, the *Reader's Digest*, the Roy M. Cohn apparatus (including Cohn creation Dennis King), the circles of the Richard Mellon-Scaife, the Associated Press, and sundry other private and official wrigglies of the "spook" world. The roster included agencies of the U.S. Joint Chiefs of Staff, that including such "Iran-Contra" spooks as Mena, Arkansas's Lt.-Col. Oliver North and Maj.-Gen. Richard Secord (ret.). Dirty Ollie North played a notable role in targetting Michael Billington: one of the facts which corrupt, intelligence-community-linked Judge Bryan did not consider suited for the jurors' tender ears.
12. Appearing before an independent body of international legal experts in September 1994, Mr. Clark said that the LaRouche case "represented a broader range of deliberate cunning and systematic misconduct over a longer period of time utilizing the power of the federal government than any other prosecution by the U.S. Government in my time or to my knowledge."

Political prisoners (left to right) Laurence Hecht, Paul Gallagher, Anita Gallagher, and Donald Phau, on Nov. 4, 1993, just before their incarceration for sentences ranging from 25 to 39 years. All are innocent. "The widespread notoriety of the wrongs in these cases, ... writes LaRouche, "calls attention to the flagrant quality of the rampant corruption within the u.s. justice system...

During 1978-1979, several U.S. citizens were targetted for fraudulent prosecution through this dirty, Holtzman-linked, political channel. In the instances of Soobzokov and LaRouche, the targetting was conduited through the *very, very dirty New York Times.* Soobzokov was to have been charged, as Demjanjuk was, but for evidence against the *Times*'s Howard Blum, showing the role of certain agencies in the same kind of solicitation of fraudulent evidence against him from the Soviet KGB which the Justice Department crafted against Demjanjuk.

The 1979 effort, by the *New York Times*, to fabricate a news-media-driven legal lynching of LaRouche, was temporarily side-tracked when investigators caught the *Times*'s Howard Blum and Paul Montgomery on recording tape, admitting to the essential features of the collaboration between the *Times* and Holtzman, among others. The exposure of the *Times* temporarily detoured its planned targetting of the present writer, which the *Times*'s represented as design to foster fraudulent prosecution against him. The *Times* turned into a side-road maintained by the notorious Roy M. Cohn, and the Cohn-controlled *Our Town* publication, all acting in concert with the Anti-Defamation League (ADL).

Soobzokov was later assassinated, in the setting of an ADL-linked hate-campaign against him; that terrorist-style murder occurred during lynch-mob demands for revenge against Soobzokov's successful civil action against the *Times* et al. The *Times*-Cohn 1979-1980 operation against LaRouche was continued as an integral part of the 1982-1983 Kissinger initiative against this writer and his associates. A related, fraudulent operation was run during the mid-1980s, through the OSI and other corrupt sections of the Justice Department's Criminal Division, against Austria's President, former UNO Secretary General Kurt Waldheim.

Among the OSI cases run by the corrupt Criminal Division (under Deputy Assistant Attorneys General John "Jack" Keeney and Mark Richard) the Demjanjuk case is notable for both its flagrancy, and for the fact that, in that case, the Criminal Division was fully exposed by Federal courts, as a down and dirty sink-hole of political corruption. The record shows, that from 1978 into the early 1990s, that Criminal Division, all the time knowing that Demjanjuk was innocent of the charges it was pressing against him, sought to bring about Demjanjuk's death, and, even today, still refuses to acknowledge that its case was a fraud from beginning to end, despite a land-mark ruling against the Department's "fraud upon the court" in that case, by the Sixth Circuit, and despite the U.S. Supreme Court's rejection of the Justice Department's attempted appeal of the Sixth Circuit decision.[13]

The flagrantly racialist conduct of the FBI and U.S. Department of Justice's Criminal Division, in the so-

---

13. See Sept. 1, 1995 testimony by Demjanjuk's Israeli attorney, Yoram Sheftel, *Independent Hearings To Investigate Misconduct by the U.S. Department of Justice* (Washington, D.C.: Schiller Institute, October 1995), pp. 49-56.

called "Frühmenschen" targetting of elected African-American officials,[14] indicates the scope of the pervasive stink of the political corruption of justice in these United States today. A glance at the overall effect, completes the essential case showing pervasive corruption in the U.S. Justice system.

As a by-product of his own victimization by such political corruption in that U.S. Department of Justice, the present writer has a significant, if partial view of the extent of wrong-doing by our Federal prosecutors and courts.

Although, the writer can say, fairly, that probably ninety-five percent, or perhaps more, of the Federal prisoners in custody had relevant apparent culpability, relatively few were convicted and sentenced by procedures deserving of the name of "due process." "Winning team" expediency by score-conscious prosecutors and courts, not justice, was the attributable motive in the majority of convictions sampled, especially under the reign of the lunatic "sentencing guidelines" legislation. Corrupt "plea-bargaining" helped unscrupulous prosecutors rack up tallies in the hits and runs columns, but also helped the "big fish" escape the charges due them, through trade-offs of those "little fish" who often serve long sentences in their stead. The sentencing guidelines, and Federal abandonment of all meaningful programs of rehabilitation of convicts, work to the worst effect on the families, and the communities from which the convicted "little fish" are taken.

The apparent general conclusion which might be offered, respecting the current state of criminal justice, overall, is that the skyrocketting, post-Nixon rate of Federal and state convictions, per 100,000 of population, suggests that, as of 1989, prior to Ambassador Robert Strauss's dispatch to Moscow, the United States' citizens had become, arguably, either the most criminally inclined people of this planet, or a people afflicted with the most corrupt criminal justice system. This writer's opinion, is that there is more than a bit of truth to both those possible inferences. Notably, the blend of post-1963 spread of the drug-culture, and spread of poverty-linked cultural pessimism, have increased the incidence of criminality in our population, while that drug-polluted pessimism and propensity for criminality, has been increased by the manifest political corruption of the criminal justice system.

Nothing contributes more efficiently to the infectious spread of a criminal disposition, than the perception, "There ain't no justice, no-how."

So, when some demagogue seeking election prattles about "Upholding the law," ask him, "Which law? Whose law?" How can one speak of "law" in unctuous terms of reference, when, by use of law, Speaker of the House Newt Gingrich's "Contract on Americans," is determined to kill many among those Americans whom the Nazis' code would have identified as "useless eaters"—unwanted children, the aged, the indigent sick, and so on—just as Hitler's Nazis would have done, also by rule of law, back during the 1930s, or as Reform Party Presidential pre-candidate Richard Lamm proposes still today? The U.S. law today stinks of corruption; the wonder is: Which is worse on that account, the negligent way in which the legislatures make law, or the manner in which the prosecutors and courts purport to enforce the statutes? Who is the honest citizen, and which is the criminal? These days, the official answer may depend upon the whim of the law-maker, the corruptly zealous, politically motivated prosecutor, or a court which has forgotten what "law" used to mean.

Whose Law Shall We Obey?

Who shall protect our nation and its people from what has become such a corrupt system of justice? The practical side of the matter requires the relevant remedies available to President and Congress, combined: Two branches of our Federal government, acting with support of the citizenry, are required, under our Federal Constitution, to clean up the erring third branch. The President, with the support of Congress, can clean out the pus from the present Justice Department; together, they can clean up the Federal courts. As our nation's earlier history has shown, once over those hills, the work proceeds easier.

However, to clear the vision of the President, the legislators, and the citizens, in such matters, the assistance of statesmen and philosophers is required. Consider the observations contained here as written with the author's authority of a statesman and philosopher, in that Leibniz tradition upon which our 1776 Declaration of Independence and 1789 Federal Constitution were premised.

We submit and examine the proposition, that the root of the general corruption of U.S. law, and our Justice system, can be accounted for, almost entirely, by the popularity of that philosophy of law, John Locke's empiricism, against which the U.S. Federal Republic

---

14. ibid.

Spokesmen for Confederate "justice" in America. Associate Justice Antonin Scalia (left) and Justice Hugo Black (right). Black is the forerunner of the kind of "democratic" lynch-mob justice to be expected from today's radical "neo-conservative" followers of John Locke.

was constituted. The apology for such types of empiricism, by Justice Antonin Scalia, identifies, with Scalia's customary cleverness, the nature of the moral depravity rampant in today's justice system.

In a recent public statement, Justice Scalia defended that presently pervasive corruption. He purported to justify such immoral practices, in both law-making and the judicial system, with the argument that such arrangements in law must be tolerated, because they are "democratic":

> "I do not know how you can argue on the basis of democratic theory that the government has a moral obligation to do something that is opposed by the people.
>
> "If the people, for example, want abortion, that state should permit abortion, in a democracy. If the people do not want it, the state should be able to prohibit it as well....
>
> "To talk about the natural law is not to talk about something we all agree upon."[15]

In choosing that line of argument, Justice Scalia adopted a philosophy of law premised upon an even more radical positivism than the notorious system of justice under the pre-World War II period of the Adolf Hitler government in Germany. Whereas the Nazi system of Carl Schmitt, et al., was derived from the Romantic school of law of G.W.F. Hegel's crony, the neo-Kantian Professor Karl Savigny, Scalia's argument is a more radically barbaric form of positivism, the form derived from both the irrationalist, "Life, Liberty, and Property" dogma of England's John Locke, and the moral indifferentism of Friedrich von Hayek's Bernard Mandeville.[16]

Scalia might thus lay claim to a Woodrow Wilson award from Nashville: The Locke doctrine which Scalia espouses, was summoned by the Confederacy, and by the Ku Klux Klan which Wilson and Hollywood's Sam Goldwyn apotheosized, to defend the institution of chattel slavery.[17]

Mention of the role of Locke's corrupting influence within the law-making and judicial practices of English-speaking North America, warns us, that the roots of Scalia's wild-eyed doctrine reach back centuries. The emphasis upon the Ku Klux Klan is eminently relevant, nonetheless: the present form of the problem which Scalia's argument typifies, dates to that specific degen-

---

15. "Scalia Says State Should Allow Abortion If Majority Wants It," by John Travis, *Arlington Catholic Herald*, Arlington, Virginia, May 16, 1996, p. 12. Scalia made the remarks on May 2 at a Rome conference sponsored by Gregorian University.

16. This comparison of Nazi and Lockean forms of radical positivism in law, was suggested, during early 1989, by one of Europe's leading legal authorities, the late Professor Friedrich von der Heydte, who also pointed out the almost exact parallels between the politically motivated, Alexandria, Virginia Federal prosecution of LaRouche, Billington, et al., and France's politically motivated, fraudulent conviction of Captain Dreyfus.

17. Hollywood moguls Samuel Goldwyn and Louis Mayer, of later Metro-Goldwyn-Mayer notoriety, played sundry leading roles in the production and distribution of the first Hollywood feature-length film, originally released under the title of *The Clansman*, subsequently renamed *The Birth of a Nation*. This film was praised, from the U.S. Executive Mansion, by President Woodrow Wilson. Wilson's endorsement became the signal for a revival of the Ku Klux Klan, reaching an estimated 4.5 millions persons during the course of the 1920s.

eration of the Federal justice system, the which came to the surface when Ku Klux Klan Kleagle Hugo Black covered his white Klan robes with the black robes of a Supreme Court Justice.

How could it be otherwise? The notable U.S. expressions of tendencies toward fascism, have always been rooted either in Romantic recollections of the Confederacy's "Lost Cause," or a spirit akin to that. We may speak of "Nashville Romanticism": *every man his own lost cause*. Typical is such corn-cob, lynch-mob "democracy" as the "I vote to string him up" tradition of populist fanaticism, traced through Confederate General and early Ku Klux Klan leader Bedford Forrest, from the political trial and execution of Socrates.[18] The most mass-murderous of the pro-fascist tendencies on the U.S. political scene today, Newt Gingrich's congressional "Critter Company," are typified by populist deserters from the Democratic Party, like ex-Georgian ex-Democrat Phil Gramm, whom the Republican Party's "Southern Strategy" picked up cheap at a Boll Weevil auction. It should be "Kristol clear," that so-called "Democrat" Hugo Black is the relevant forerunner of the kind of "democratic" lynch-justice to be expected from today's radical, "neo-conservative" followers of John Locke.

The Church-State Issue

How is it, that so many Americans seem to have overlooked the pungent body-odor of such uncivilized "Critters"?

There are two leading, immediate issues presented by Justice Hugo Black's role in fostering the present degeneration of U.S. law-making and justice. The relatively more superficial issue was Black's doctrine, of separation of not only church, but also Christian morality, from law, the latter a view which Jefferson held, in opposition to the U.S. Federal Constitution. The deeper question is: If Black were axiomatically in error constitutionally, as he was, by what standard should we judge whether the relevant principle inhering in that Constitution were correct?

Let us begin at the surface, as were one some noble, dedicated dog, digging vermin out from under the pasture: Hugo Black's insistence that the Bill of Rights prescribes an absolute separation of church from state. Black cited Jefferson as his authority for this opinion. Was Black accurate respecting Jefferson's opinion? Yes. Black's fraud lay in his two-fold sleight-of-hand: he substituted the intent of Bill of Rights sponsor, the eccentric, anti-Federalist Jefferson, for the intent of those, Jefferson's political opponents of that time, who crafted the Federal Constitution over his objection.[19]

As Philip Valenti and others have documented this fact, the post-1688 conspiracy leading to the 1776-1783 U.S. War of Independence, was rooted in the American patriot's choice of Gottfried Leibniz, in opposition to that of Jefferson's and the later Confederacy's guru, John Locke.[20] This is typified by the appearance, in the 1776 U.S. Declaration of Independence, of "life, liberty, and the pursuit of happiness," in explicit rejection of John Locke's "life, liberty, and property."[21]

The *Federalist Papers*, and Tom Paine's warning against democracy's use as a substitute for republican principles of law, illustrate the point: the founders of our Federal republic relied upon a view of history rooted in Classical Greece. Otherwise, some of the bitterest memories and deepest fears of our Eighteenth-century patriots, were focussed upon the lessons of the Venice-orchestrated, ruinous, religious wars of the Sixteenth and Seventeenth Centuries.[22] Our patriots shared

---

18. Lynch-mob democracy does not limit its choice of burnt offerings to African-American scape-goats. During the period of the 1996 primary campaigns, this writer had the opportunity, as a Democratic Presidential candidate, in various "candidates events," during some of which he witnessed the arguments of candidates for criminal-appeals justices and prosecutors' positions. Notable, and disgusting, was the frequency with which rivals were denounced for "voting their conscience, rather than giving the public what it wants:" that is nakedly lynch-justice, like some Supreme Court rulings which Justice Scalia co-sponsored.

19. Hugo Black's Jeffersonian view of the U.S. Constitution finds support in the revisionist theory of history presented by the British-trained socialist, Charles Beard. Beard mimics Jefferson's hostility to Federalism in his own venomous libel against the 1787-1789 drafting of the Federal Constitution.

20. Phil Valenti, *EIR*, Dec. 1, 1995, "The Anti-Newtonian Roots of the American Revolution." On the origins and initial formation of this American conspiracy, see H. Graham Lowry, *How The Nation Was Won* (Washington, D.C.: EIR, 1987), passim. On the historical root of the factional divisions between patriots and American Tories within North America, see Anton Chaitkin, *Treason in America*, 2nd cd., (New York City: New Benjamin Franklin House, 1986).

21. G.W. Leibniz, *Society & Economy*, J. Chambless, trans., *Fidelio*, Fall 1992, pp. 54. Also, G.W. Leibniz, *New Essays Concerning Human Understanding*, A.G. Langley, trans. (Chicago: Open Court, 1949). On the meaning of Leibniz's use of the term "happiness," see below.

22. Not only were the Plantagenet Cardinal Pole and Thomas Cromwell, like Francesco Zorzi, assets deployed in Tudor England by Venice. The prolonged war for independence of the Netherlands is another outstanding case. What the marytred Henry IV of France had delayed, became the 1618-1648 "Thirty Years War" sought by Venice's powerful Paolo Sarpi. The spillover of the Thirty Years War into Britain, supplied a new dimension to religious warfare there.

bitter reflections upon the bloodied history of the Established Church of England. In sum, the founders of the U.S.A. were profoundly committed to the axiomatic features of western-European Christian civilization, but fearfully opposed to the existence of an *established church*.[23]

For their attempted resolution of the intertwined problems of established church and religious wars, the founders of the U.S.A. were influenced chiefly by the ecumenical thinking of G.W. Leibniz. In sum, the state should not be controlled by the sectarian doctrines of a particular church, but must be controlled, nonetheless, by the moral principles inherent in *natural law*. It is this natural law on which the principal founders of the United States premised that Federal constitutional republic, to whose establishment Jefferson had been opposed.

That is the backdrop, against which to judge the essential folly permeating the referenced doctrines of Hugo Black and Antonin Scalia.

The natural law is comprised of those moral principles, including notions of God, and relationship between God and man, which might be adduced with scientific certainty, although no religious text had ever been written. The twisted mind of the fanatical sectarian sometimes denounces this view of "natural law," as allegedly "Deism," as an affront to those mystical claims which are often represented as tenets of this or that private-labelling of "revealed religion."[24] No one

had made the principle of natural law clearer to the founders of our republic than Leibniz. Like Leibniz, the circles associated with Cotton Mather and Benjamin Franklin recognized, that the superiority of the modern, western European model of nation-state republic, over other choices of organization of society, had been derived, as Augustine of Hippo had stipulated, from the application of Christian principles to the Classical Greek designs of Solon and Plato. They viewed the coincidence of a secular body of natural law with Christianity, accordingly.[25]

Thus, to introduce the paganist model of separation of church from state, in the form advocated by Justices Hugo Black, Antonin Scalia, et al., would mean to exclude the presumption, at law, of any demonstrable, axiomatic authority for any *moral principles which coincide with those of Christianity*. Scalia, for example, has drawn precisely that presumption from his radical-positivist's perversion of "democracy." He states, that he is willing to allow Christian opinion to persuade a democratic majority among law-makers, but he prohibits the attribution of any axiomatic principle of morality to the body of law. In this respect, Scalia is a neo-Cartesian, a radical positivist of a relatively extremist disposition.

Leibniz's relevant comments on articles 37 and 39 of the first part of René Descartes' *Principles* illustrate the point. We cite from the Schrecker translation.[26]

To Descartes' "37. Man's greatest perfection is the power of free will, and this is what renders him worthy of praise or blame," Leibniz responded as follows:

> "On *Article 37*. Man's greatest perfection is to act [according to reason],[27] no less than to act

---

23. This would implicitly prevent Mr. Reed's so-called "Christian Coalition" from arrogating to itself the functions of an "established church." In any case, while Mr. Reed's arch-hypocritical crew might pretend merely to defend foetuses, it is often, like allies Oliver North and Newt Gingrich's "Contract on Americans," indifferent, or even homicidal, respecting the lives of such matured foetuses as pregnant mothers and the aged. Granted, some would interpret the referenced patriotic views on "established church" as echoing the "conciliar" movement which dominated the pre-Florence councils of early the Fifteenth Century; ecumenist Gottfried Leibniz, and his followers, did not support the democratic notions of the "left-wing" "conciliar" tradition."

24. On the contrary, as the Gospel of St. John and the Epistles of St. Paul make clear to all who are literate, the Apostolic Christian tradition based itself on the authority of Plato's view of natural law. The point is, that Christianity is premised not on simple-minded, symbolic reading of excerpted texts of Scripture, but rather upon those truths of Christian teaching which reason will not contradict. Unlike the lunacy of the Nostradamus cult, Christianity is not based on magical interpretations of supposed prophecy, but upon its authority as demonstrably truthful according to the principle of reason. It is of special importance, that none of the forms of irrationalist belief in magical recipes, as associated with sectarian cults, be imposed upon the state; but, this does not mean that Kleagle Hugo Black's cult of anti-Christian secularism should replace

the natural law which reason finds embedded in Christian morality.

25. Although natural law may not incorporate all that sundry factions of Judaism or Islam might wish to incorporate as law, no leading current derived from the monotheism of Moses would exclude the authority of the natural law as natural law were competently defined, for example, by western Christianity. Thus, a republic, such as the U.S.A. was founded to be, is intrinsically a suitable sort of ecumenical habitat for any branch of Moses' monotheism. As Leibniz stressed, this ecumenicism extends implicitly to the heritage of Confucius and Mencius in China.

26. G.W. Leibniz, *Monadology and Other Philosophical Essays*, Paul and Anne Martin Schrecker, trans. (New York City: MacMillan Publishing Co., 1965), pp. 34-35. The passages from the Schrecker translation have been slightly amended by this writer, on the authority of his own deep familiarity with Leibniz's method of thinking, and his abhorrence of the want of civilized punctuation in prevailing, illiterate conventions of the *New York Times* and other current arbiters of English prose style.

27. The Schrecker translation reads "to act reasonably," which is an un-

freely; or, rather, the two are one and the same, since he is the more free, the less the use of his reason is troubled by the influence of [erotic—LHL] passion."[28]

To Descartes' "39. That our free will is known without proof, solely by our experience of it." Leibniz replies:

"*On Article 39.* To ask whether freedom depends upon our will, is the same as to ask whether our will depends upon our will. For 'free' and 'voluntary' mean the same. Freedom is spontaneity directed by reason, and, 'to will,' is to be carried into action by reasons perceived by the intellect. Action is free, in proportion as reason is pure, and unclouded by brute and confused perceptions...."

For Leibniz, the principles of reason govern the will of the civilized, moral person, in a sense analogous to the selection of those theorems of geometry which do not violate consistency with the relevant hypothesis (i.e., axioms, postulates, definitions) underlying that choice of geometry, taken as a whole. By "reason," or "necessary and sufficient reason," Leibniz, like Plato and Johannes Kepler before him, means much more than a mere formal logic. His Platonic use of the term, "reason," signifies the faculty by means of which mankind has been able to replace both fallible and insufficient axioms, postulates, and definitions, with measur-

ably valid (e.g., superior, efficacious) alternate notions of governing principle.[29]

Thus, for Leibniz, as for the present writer, morality is not some list of "do's and don't's," posted, like "ukases," in the Czar's village square. Morality is located in those discernible principles of our universe (axioms), the which must govern our construction and adoption of those propositions which we select to serve as the theorems of obligation and prohibition.

Granted, in the widespread practice of religion, the believer has often been a simple fellow who assumes that his church has worked out such a reasonable selection of moral theorems, as doctrine. Sometimes, that necessary, higher authority, which he follows blindly, is correct, in greater or lesser degree. However, the fact, that blind faith in higher authority, as such, may provide just guidance in some cases, must not be summoned as premise for the sophistry, that the authority which might be attributable to a moral teaching is itself rooted axiomatically in blind faith.

The immorality of Justice Scalia's argument, is shown most efficiently by treating his arguments for "democracy" as the kind of Cartesian tradition whose folly Leibniz exposed in the cited references above. The "freedom" which our Federal Republic's founders defended, was not the Hobbesian idea of "freedom," of war of each against all, as suggested by Descartes, John Locke, and Adam Smith.[30] "Freedom" is not license to

---

Leibnizian rendering. To act according to reason, as Leibniz defines "necessary and sufficient reason," is Leibniz's intent in all locations where this point is addressed by him, not the misuse of the term "reasonably" as commonly employed by the corruption which passes for today's English prose style.

28. Since the Classical Greek of Plato, as carried over into the usages of St. Paul's Epistles, two distinct qualities of emotion are recognized. *Eros* (erotic passion), in both its sexual and other connotations, pertains to the passions associated with distinct objects of sense-perception (whether actual or merely fancied). *Agapē*, conventionally translated into Latin as *Caritas*, or the King James' *Charity*, signifies for Plato the quality associated with love for truth, and love for Justice. This also signifies "love of God," "love of mankind," and those ideas which exist only as *Platonic ideas* of scientific knowledge, as distinct from directly perceptible sense-objects. Thus, we must distinguish *agapic* passion, as passion for truthfulness respecting principles of reason, from the *erotic* passions of strict materialism and empiricism. See the text, below, for relevant references to the natural-law significance of this distinction.

29. Putting aside some sloppy definitions supplied by certain putative "authorities," Leibniz's use of "necessary and sufficient reason" (where mechanistic thinkers employ "cause") is situated in his pervasive reliance upon Plato's Socratic *method of hypothesis*. An hypothesis is the interdependent set of axioms, postulates, and definitions, the which underlie any not-inconsistent *theorem-lattice* (i.e., array of known and possible theorems which are mutually not-inconsistent throughout the array). The set of axioms, postulates, and definitions satisfying that requirement for a theorem-lattice, is an *hypothesis*. Given, for example, any discovered physical principle shown to be valid by means of crucial kind of experimental measurement. Given, then, a crucial event within a physical geometry cohering with that principle. In that case, as Bernhard Riemann's method argues, the *hypothesis* incorporating that principle serves as the identifiable "necessary and sufficient reason" for any crucial event occurring within that physical geometry. Classical examples of this include, the coherence ("general relativity") which Jean Bernoulli and Leibniz demonstrated, between isochronicity in the gravitational field, and refraction of light at constant retarded potential for propagation of light. This typifies Leibniz's refined application of Kepler's employment of "reason."

30. Adam Smith's apology for Bernard Mandeville's absolute immorality of "free will," first appears in print in Smith's 1759 *Theory of the Moral Sentiments*, and as the doctrine of the "Invisible Hand," in

Rene Descartes (left) and Gottfried Leibniz (above). The "freedom" which our Federal Republic's founders defended, was the freedom of Leibniz, based on reason—not the Hobbesian idea of "freedom," of war of each against ali, advocated by Descartes.

follow one's whims at society's expense. "Freedom" is the obligation and right to act according to *reason*, as the scientists Kepler and Leibniz defined the use of the terms *reason* and *necessary and sufficient reason*. It is the obligation and freedom to act as such reason demands we act, even, when, "in the course of human events," this signifies morally obligatory defiance of an unjust political or financier authority.

The positivist doctrine in law, either as Scalia's view of "democracy," or, the same doctrine in its anti-democratic guise, as Nazi law, is always intrinsically immoral, precisely because the doctrine rejects the obligations of reason, because it insists that morality consists in nothing other than obeying established covenants of positive law, ethics, or Kant's and Savigny's notions of custom.[31] For unfortunates such as Scalia, as was the case for the Nazi government, the enactment of even a single, arbitrary law, can change radically the mandatory morality of an entire nation. Precisely so, in the relevant case of first impression, did mass-murderers in

the 1946 Nuremberg proceedings attempt to justify their crimes against humanity, as according to the prevailing law at that time. So, did morally corrupted U.S. courts uphold the "Jim Crow" system of such pro-Confederacy Presidents as Theodore Roosevelt and Woodrow Wilson.

Just so, have apologists for today's Nuremberg-style criminal, Pennsylvania Governor Tom Ridge, who purported to excuse Ridge's fully witting crimes against humanity. The Pennsylvania-born Nuremberg prosecutor, U.S. Supreme Court Justice Robert Jackson, and Philadelphia's Nuremberg-Trial Judge Francis Biddle, upheld the principle under which Ridge is to be adjudged guilty of a Nazi-style crime. The relevant doctrines of Scalia and of the Nazi regime are, thus, efficiently equal in this respect.

The founders of our republic would have agreed with this writer, and with Leibniz: that, were we to attempt to make such a radical separation of morality from law, as Scalia does, we would virtually ensure, as the German supporters of Hitler did earlier, the early ruin of our nation, plunging us all into the chaos such folly had brought upon us and our posterity.

Admittedly, out of fairness to Justice Scalia, we must give the Devil his proverbial due. In the alternative, were we to impose upon the state the contemptible hypocrisy of Reed's Christian Coalition, to prohibit abortions, but to tolerate "conservatives" who demand "triage" of "useless eaters" (as by means of mass-murder of aged, sick, and poor, such as economic-austerity measures in the cause of "free trade" ideology), we would be imitating thus, *exactly*, those criminal, but *aggressively pro-natalist* policies which the mass-mur-

---

Smith's 1776, anti-American tract, *The Wealth of Nations*.

31. e.g., Custom: *Zeitgeist, Volksgeist*.

Ovens at the Dachau concentration camp. Inset: Pennsylvania Gov. Tom Ridge. The Nuremberg prosecutors "upheld the principle under which Ridge is to be adjudged guilty of a Nazi-style crime. The relevant doctrines of Scalia and of the Nazi regime are, thus, efficiently equal in this respect."

derous Adolf Hitler regime began during the 1930s. The point is, that the so-called Christian Coalition, like Antonin Scalia, operates under the governance of *no consistent moral principle*, but, rather, relies upon the self-righteous hypocrite's "single-theorem" sophistry. One suspects that they would overlook Adolf Hitler's gas chambers for the sake of unity against abortion; there is no Adolf Hitler presently available to test that proposition, but Reed's Christian Coalition has found a serviceable surrogate in Newt Gingrich's "Contract on Americans"—to impose upon Gingrich's flock the title demanded by "truth in advertising" policies.

Both Justice Scalia and the Christian Coalition share a common lack of moral principle: the sophist's *method* in law; Scalia's relative moral advantage, over the Christian Coalition,[32] is, that he has confessed his immorality to be such, publicly, whereas, Reed's Christian Coalition wants Scalia's candor.

Like the radical, land-grabbing, Zionist zealots who assassinated Israel's Prime Minister Yitzhak Rabin, Reed's Coalition demonstrates the menace in permitting the state to be subjected to "the revealed dogma" of hypocritical sophists. Thus, the Constitution's appended Bill of Rights is correct, in requiring the separa-

tion of the state's law-making from the caprices of sectarian religious bodies, such as Reed's array of sententious hypocrites. Nonetheless, having once given the Devil his due, Hugo Black and his followers, such as Justice Scalia, were flagrantly immoral, in deriving from a doctrine of separation of "state from an established church," the inconsequential, irrelevant, immoral, and unlawful dogma, of separating the morality of non-sectarian *natural law* from the axiomatic moral basis which must control all law-making.

No thoughtful Christian could sustain an objection to this. The essence of Christianity is the quality of evangelism stressed by Paul's *I Corinthians* 13. Without *agapē*, all supposed moralizing, or putative good deeds, are without credit to the actor. Without *agapē*, the doer of a good deed is no better than a millstone, which grinds the grain without being itself spiritually ennobled. It is winning people to love of that quality of truthful principle suited to *agapē*, and practicing that principle, which is the Christian's concern. To defend reason and life, in all human manifestations, is a principle of natural law, which must be served indivisibly, without sophist's quibbling. It is the principle of natural law, which the Christian will recognize as the issue to be taken up against such pagan Justices as Hugo Black and Antonin Scalia.

The point is, no church has the intrinsic authority to impose what morality shall be respecting the law of the

---

32. From Brother Reed's performance to date, one might speculate, that the original "Christian Coalition" were a Princeton University-style eating club, organized by the lions of pagan Rome's Colosseum.

nation-state, *if that determination be contrary to a clear and distinct foundation in a body of natural law derived from nothing but reason.* Scalia is right, therefore, to insist that the law must not be premised upon what mere "blind faith" decrees to be morality. Scalia is in grave error, in omitting the merely positive law's obligatory submission to the higher authority of reason, of natural law.

Lest there be some doubt of the necessity of natural law: In place of religious blind faith, Scalia substitutes the panic of the heathen mob drunk with its own assortment of blind passions. Scalia replaces the church with the corrupting, erotic passions of satanic Bernard Mandeville's pleasure-palace, and wicked Adam Smith's market-place; in matters of law, Scalia is a communicant of the pagan low church of Friedrich Nietzsche's and Martin Heidegger's *Dionysos*. The latter is a church which must, indeed, be separated from our state.

Obviously, if a church has command of the principles of natural law, then it must be acknowledged as a proper, expert counsellor of the state, on that account. However, rewards in Heaven, and punishment in Hell, must be determined in courts which are capable of efficiently awarding those destinies, not earthly courts. We mortals have enough on our hands, in administering a natural law whose matters can be heard in our earthly courts, were those courts moral ones. As eyewitnesses Michael Billington and Jacques Cheminade can expertly attest, to find an honest earthly court to hear earthly matters, under the law condoned by the highest courts, in Scalia's U.S.A., or Jacques Chirac's France, today, already partakes of the miraculous.

Before leaving the matter of church and state, there remains an additional, major consideration, under this heading, which must be identified now. Today, the role of natural law per se—as distinct from a confessional doctrine—has a far more immediate practical importance for the United States, than at any earlier time.

Modern, western-European civilization, of which all of the nations of the Americas are expressions, was developed under the influence of western Christianity. Were we to abandon that Christian culture, our societies would collapse rapidly. Yet, the world of the future is centered in the Eurasia continent, where East and South Asia represent approximately half the population of the world. The most populous religious cultural matrices of the region, are not Christian, but Islamic, Confucian, Hindu, or Buddhist. Islam, as a branch of Mosaic monotheism, is more readily accessible to the comprehension of the western European. As Leibniz was the first to demonstrate, there are subtle, but powerful cultural affinities, respecting natural law, between western Christianity and the Confucian heritage.[33]

To the degree these religious-cultural differences can be bridged, and not all can be readily bridged, it is only from the standpoint of natural law that this could be accomplished. The point may be clarified by proposing here, that natural law may also be identified, with some qualification, as "ecumenical law," not in the sense of pragmatists such as William James, but in Leibniz' sense of the matter, or that of Nicolaus of Cusa, earlier. The implications of this will become clearer as we summarize the scientific proof for the rudiments of a universal natural law, below.

By the applicable standards of natural law, lawmaking and courts in the U.S.A. and elsewhere today, are in a morally degraded state. Scalia's exclusion of morality has already prevailed, and the result is a catastrophe. He were better advised to reflect on reversing the calamities produced by his own savagely erroneous present opinion, than to continue to justify that recipe, Hugo Black's and his own, which has produced such inedible dishes.

If those lines of argument made here thus far, be granted, there remains an important, additional hurdle, yet to be surmounted: How shall we determine, with scientific certitude, what should be recognized as constituting the *natural law*? We turn now to that matter.

Physical Economy and Natural law

As we have presented that evidence, in various earlier locations, a study of the demography of Earth, within the setting of the ecological conditions existing during the recent two millions years, suffices to prove three crucial principles.

First, the increase of mankind's potential population-density, and also our species' improved life-expectancy and productivity, demonstrates, that the human individual is set absolutely apart from, and superior to all other living species, as *Genesis* 1:26-30 argues.

Second, a retrospective view of the improve-

---

33. "Discourse on the Natural Theology of the Chinese (1716)" in *Gottfried Wilhelm Leibniz, Writings on China*, edited by Daniel J. Cook and Harry Rosemont, Jr. (Peru, Illinois: Open Court Publishing Co., 1994).

ment in human demography, referenced to the post-1461 establishment
of the modern, western European
form of nation-state, shows that this
improvement in demography, is the
consequence of the combination of
general education, with the fostering,
through means of the individual
mind's creative, cognitive processes,
of scientific, technological, and related discoveries of principle. It is
nothing other than this creative potential, typified by valid discoveries and
employment of principles of nature
for scientific and technological progress, which sets mankind apart from,
and above all other species.

Third, that the struggle which defines human history, to date, is between the efforts to establish a form of
state based upon universal education
for ongoing scientific and related
progress, and against the evil heritage
of so-called "traditionalist" and oli-
garchical (e.g., feudal-aristocratic, fi-
nancier-aristocratic) forms of society,
such as those conforming with the evil
Code of the Emperor Diocletian.

*LaRouche associate Jacques Cheminade (right) campaigns for the French
Presidency in April 1995. Cheminade has been subjected to a travesty of justice
in France, which parallels that of Billington et al. in the United States. On Aug.
2, the French government seized his bank account, in a ludicrous attempt to
collect the million francs in matching funds that the state had advanced for his
Presidential campaign. Now that the campaign is over, and the money spent, the
government is demanding that he personally return the funds.*

Thus far, those three principles can be demonstrated
by no more than appropriate application of the methods
of experimental physics. We must not start with any
choice of formal mathematics, but only the principle of
measurement, as Nicolaus of Cusa laid down the foundations of modern European science in his *De docta
ignorantia.*[34] An appropriate mathematics must not be
adopted until after the crucial measurements have been
completed. A rigorous proof of the existence of these
three principles requires measurements must be made
in terms of the branch of physical science known as
physical economy.[35]

The emphasis upon physical economy signifies,
among other implications, that money, credit, and debt,
have never existed except in the form of political fictions, and that any effort to derive a theory of economy
based on such measurements in such units (or upon the
related political fictions of "marginal utility"), must
lead to absurdities. Competence begins by rejecting any
assumption implying that the function of "economics"
is to present a "theory of business."[36] Economics must
signify reliance upon physical facts (such as products,
market-baskets of physical goods, etc.), and upon necessary *physical principles* adduced by crucial experimental demonstrations of proof based upon such facts.

The central significant fact of physical-economic
measurements of societies taken as indivisible wholes,
is that this approach enables us to demonstrate, by the
standards of experimental physics, both certain princi-

---

34. Cardinal Nicolaus of Cusa, *De Docta Ignorantia (On Learned Ignorance)*, translated by Jasper Hopkins as *Nicholas of Cusa on Learned
Ignorance* (Minneapolis, Minnesota: Arthur J. Banning Press, 1985).

35. For an introductory textbook in physical economy: Lyndon H. La-
Rouche, Jr., *So, You Wish to Learn All About Economics?* (Washington,
D.C.: EIR, 1995). That text provides an adequate guide for the reader
with a background in any branch of engineering which employs the
methods of input-output measurements based upon process sheets, bills

of materials, and market-baskets.

36. Rather, "business" should be judged as an optional function of
physical economy, for reasons to be stressed below.

ples of the human cognitive processes, and certain corresponding, general principles of nature. Furthermore, in this way, we are able to obtain relevant measurements, by means of which to prove certain crucial, subsidiary principles. The result is meaningfully termed "natural law," in the sense that natural law signifies the way in which both mankind, and the universe, have been *manifestly pre-designed to function, and to interact.* That may be restated: *Natural Law is the hypothesis which corresponds to the necessary and sufficient reason for mankind's successfully continued existence.*

Consider next, the general characteristic of successful human existence. The approach of experimental physics, shows us a most crucial general principle, underlying the growth of human population under conditions of both increased per-capita productivity, and improved demographic characteristics.

The level of potential physical productivity of a society, per capita, per household. and per relevant square kilometer of the Earth's surface, depends both upon a certain development of the human intellect, and also certain minimal standards of both demographic characteristics and consumption. The consumption includes a standard of *functionally necessary* household consumption, functionally-necessary consumption for necessary basic economic infrastructure, and functionally-necessary consumption for production and related functions of output of goods. This minimal level of requirement is increased, in terms of knowledge, and of demographic and market-basket requirements, as the transition to a higher general level of potential physical productivity is made.[37]

This notion of functionally-determined minimum levels, is conveniently deposited under the schoolbook heading: "Energy of the System." The introduction of that notion, obliges us to consider the function associated with society's output in excess of "Energy of the System" requirements, obviously the function of "Free Energy." However, since advancement requires "investment" in higher per-capita and per-square-kilometer rates of "Energy of the System," it might appear to a schoolboy not familiar with economics, that the ratio of "Free Energy" to "Energy of the System" must decline as relative "capital intensity" is increased through technological progress. On the contrary, in all successful cases, the ratio of "Free Energy" to "Energy of the System" does not decline, despite the increase in the "Energy of the System" per capita, per household, and per square kilometer. This latter performance may be termed "The Not-Entropy of the Economic Process," i.e., a defiance of the so-called "Law of Entropy."

Thus, Leibniz's (and U.S. Treasury Secretary Alexander Hamilton's[38]) notion of *the productive powers of labor* is expressed in an interdependency of two measurable terms: a) ratio of free energy to energy of the system, and, b) energy of the system per capita, per household, and per square kilometer for the society considered functionally as an indivisible whole. The productive powers of labor of the individual within that society, are a function of the impact of the activity of that individual, upon the productive characteristics of the society as a functional unity.

The implied "isotherm" for productive powers of labor (per capita, per household, and per square kilometer), is expressed by the inequalities indicated above: a) the ratio of "free energy" to "energy of the system" must be significantly greater than "zero," and not decline; b) the "energy of the system" (per capita, per household, per square kilometer) must increase.

The notion expressed by that pair of inequalities, is premised, inclusively, upon the physical demonstration, that continued output in a fixed mode, incurs the "entropic" effects of marginalized resources. This suggests that scientific, technological, and related expressions of progress, is mandatory, and that a policy of the type implied by "zero technological progress" is suicidal, is not an available option for any survivable mode of human existence. That is to say, that the potential relative population-density, demographic characteristics, and quality of individual daily life of the society, must degenerate under the influence of such a policy.

This demonstration leads to a corresponding, generalized, functional notion of "technological attrition."

The fact that successful existence of the human species depends upon such a "not-entropic" result, achieved through scientific and related progress in generalized social practice, prompts us to regard that "not-entropic" function we have identified here, as of extraordinary significance. That significance may be expressed in various ways, according to the vantage-point from which we examine it. In general, we should say, that this "not-entropy," is the smiling face which the universe presents to us, when we provoke that universe

---

37. Cf. Gottfried Leibniz, *Society & Economy (1671)*, loc. cit.

38. Alexander Hamilton, *Report to the U.S. Congress: On the Subject of Manufactures*, December 1791.

with the employment of a valid, axiomatic-revolutionary discovery of principle of nature, either as a scientific principle, or as an improved technology derived from such a validated principle.

The method of experimental physics demonstrates to us, that there are valid discoveries of principle, proven to be valid by means of differences of measured effects. The human individual has the power which no other species exhibits, the power to discover and adopt revolutionary principles of change in human practice, through which the power of mankind over nature is increased, in the manner, and according to the general constraints which we have outlined above. The phenomena of technological attrition show us, that mankind's continued existence, in population-densities above those of higher apes, depends upon a continued development and employment of such radical changes in human behavior, notably those changes, throughout discernible evidence of human existence, which we class, retrospectively, or otherwise, as valid, axiomatic-revolutionary discoveries of principle, through which the behavior of a society is improved radically. In such consideration of that physical-economic evidence, we have struck upon the ore from whose refinement we may extract the purer metal of "human nature." This "ore" serves us as the evidence leading to a functional definition of *natural law*.

Agapē: How Ideas Are Communicated

We must preface the argument of the next several points with a clarifying set of definitions of certain specialist's terms employed, above, and now.

1. *Deductive argument defined.* All spoken languages, including today's generally accepted mathematics, are rendered "grammatical" by subjecting them to a kind of evolutionary principle, the which we recognize as what is claimed as formal "logical consistency," but which is more fairly, and rigorously described as "lack of apparent, logical inconsistency."

2. *Theorem.* Those selected sets of propositions, expressed in terms of such a language, which, each, are demonstrably not inconsistent with any other of the whole, may be termed *theorems* of that set.

3. *Hypothesis.* By employment of Plato's Socratic method, we are able to adduce a common set of definitions and axiomatic assumptions, the which implicitly subsume each theorem of a set of theorems. The set of underlying assumptions (definitions, axioms, and postulates, for example), is termed an *hypothesis*.

4. *Theorem-Lattice.* This hypothesis enables us to define, implicitly, an additional collection of theorems, the which would be not-inconsistent with the original set of theorems. The combination of known and possible such theorems, represents a *theorem-lattice*. A classroom Euclidean geometry, or an empiricist or Cartesian algebra, are examples of theorem-lattices.

5. *Axiomatic-revolutionary discovery of principle.* In the case, that reality demonstrates, that one or more among the constituent elements of such a formal hypothesis is false, a new hypothesis, consistent with the relevant "experimental evidence," must replace the flawed one. That validated new hypothesis, is axiomatically inconsistent with the superseded, flawed hypothesis, and, therefore, could not be derived, by means of deductive methods, from the old hypothesis. Such a validated change in axiom, and of hypothesis, is to be recognized as an *axiomatic-revolutionary discovery of principle*, or, in abbreviation, simply as a *discovery of principle*.

6. *Creative mental act.* For such a case, the means by which the validated version of a discovered, axiomatic solution is produced, is an exemplary *creative mental act*, in absolute contrast to a mental act of deduction/induction.

7. *Cognition.* This quality of creative mental act, so defined, is identified as the essential quality associated with proper use of the terms *cognition*, and *cognitive processes*.

8. *Higher hypothesis.* In actuality, today's validatable human knowledge embodies an accumulation of validated, axiomatic-revolutionary discoveries of principle, and a corresponding succession of hypotheses. In the case, that the specific method of cognition employed successfully in some sequence of validated discoveries of principle, is successfully employed for added, validated discoveries of principle continuing that sequence, we have a set of hypotheses, each superior to its predecessor, all originated in a common way. The assumptions underlying that specific method of cognition, form a type of hypothesis. This special type of hypothesis, underlies the predicated many[39] hypotheses of the sequence, as an ordinary hypothesis underlies the set of theorems of a theorem-lattice. This higher type of hy-

---

39. "Many" is employed here in the sense that Plato's *Parmenides* dialogue addresses the type of the "one-many," ontological paradox presented by considering the relationship of an underlying hypothesis to the predicated theorems of its theorem-lattice.

pothesis is termed by Plato a *higher hypothesis*.[40]

9. *Hypothesizing the higher hypothesis*. The state of cognition is of the type of higher hypothesis. This includes a special, higher type of hypothesizing which is known, from Plato, as *hypothesizing the higher hypothesis*. In this latter case, hypothesizing the higher hypothesis underlies axiomatic improvements in the scientific method represented as an higher hypothesis, or validly ordered sequence of higher hypotheses, as an higher hypothesis (e.g., experimental-scientific method of discovery of principle), similarly, underlies a valid sequence of hypotheses.

10. *Necessary and sufficient reason*. Leibniz's notion of his principle of scientific discovery, *necessary and sufficient reason*, is a reflection of those Platonic conceptions underlying the method of experimental physical science. The significance of Leibniz's principle, is recognized more adequately from the standpoint of Riemann's 1854 habilitation dissertation, which addresses the same matter from precisely the standpoint of the method of hypothesis, as referenced within the immediately foregoing definitions here.

Briefly, the case for viewing Leibniz's *necessary and sufficient reason* from the vantage-point of Riemann's principle of hypothesis, works to the following effect. If each physically validated discovery of principle, is treated as a dimension of an "n-dimensional" physical geometry (manifold), then the ordering principle corresponding to a sequence of validated such discoveries, is a type of higher hypothesis which is representable in terms of an ordering, as progression from a physical space-time manifold (geometry) of "n," to "n+1" dimensions. The crucial added feature, integral to Riemann's argument, is that the successive such physical geometries can be compared, only by departing the formalist domain of a presently generally accepted mathematical physics, for the domain of experimental physics.

> **The creative power of cognition, is functionally dependent upon an associated emotional state of the individual. To signify this emotional state, Plato and the Apostle Paul employed the term *agapē*. In Plato, we encounter this as signifying the quality of love for justice, and for truth. In *I Corinthians* 13, Paul uses *agapē*. to the same effect, as extended to love of mankind and love of God. This is the same emotion seen in the child overjoyed by its own discovery of a principle.**

The key to the success of that effort lies in the fact, that any physical geometry may be treated geodetically, in terms of the relative curvature of physical space-time associated with each. That is to say, that the difference in metrical characteristics which formally distinguish physical space-time manifolds, provides us the means for verifying a choice of manifold in the terms of an experimental physics: in the same sense that those Classical Greeks working in the tradition of scientific method represented by Plato, were able to prove a definite curvature of the Earth, more than two millennia before that curvature was known as a sense-perceptual fact.

To appreciate Leibniz's notion of *necessary and sufficient reason*, paraphrase Riemann's approach to the same subject-matter. Given: a crucial event, such as the empirical evidence of least action, in terms of the determination of refraction of light under conditions of retarded propagation. What are the constituents of the hypothesis which determines the measured experimental result to have been a necessary result? That hypothesis constitutes the "necessary" and "sufficient" reason for the relevant crucial-experimental event.

11. *Agapē*. The creative power of cognition, is functionally dependent upon an associated emotional state of the individual. To signify this emotional state, Plato and the Apostle Paul employed the term *agapē*. In Plato, we encounter this as signifying the quality of love for justice, and for truth. In *I Corinthians* 13, Paul uses *agapē* to the same effect, as extended to love of mankind and love of God. This is the same emotion seen in the child overjoyed by its own discovery of a principle. It is often described as "the light turning on" in the personality experiencing an creative act of insight, and is also the referent for "tears of joy." This is the emotion of scientific discovery, and also the emotion associated with the work of metaphor in a Classical work of art, such as a well-performed tragedy of Aeschylus, Shakespeare, or Schiller, or a well-performed principal composition of J.S. Bach, Wolfgang Mozart, Beethoven, Schubert, or Brahms: the competence of such performances depends upon the governance of the performer

---

40. Leibniz references the characteristics of such an higher hypothesis under such headings as *"analysis situs."*

by that passion peculiar to cognition, the passion of "tears of joy."

Reference *I Corinthians* 13. This writer persists in demanding the use of the original Greek *agapē*, rejecting the usual modern connotations of the conventional Latin translation, *caritas*, or the King James Version's *charity*. Paul emphasizes that none of those acts which present-day convention associates with "charity," constitute *agapē*. It is not the deed as such, which gives the merit to the doer, but rather the assertion of that specific, efficient passion for truth and justice according to reason, *agapē*, within the doer. In Leibniz's terms, *agapē* is, for Paul, integral to that *necessary and sufficient reason* for the relevant deed; it is in the axiomatic principle of *agapē*, as an integral axiom of that *necessary and sufficient reason*, that the virtue (i.e., the Renaissance's *virtù!*) lies. For a deeper insight into Paul's argument, see Plato's definition of *The Good*.

12. *The Good*. No absurdity is so pervasive in modern civilization, as the notion of points existing at "infinity," as in past and future. These ideas, sometimes appearing in their guise as "limit theory," correspond to no reality which ever did, or ever could exist; but these foolish ideas cause much trouble, in many ways, not only in theology, but also mathematics, and in science generally. For our purposes here, it is sufficient to define, summarily, the relevant aspects of the relationship among *hypothesis* and Plato's notion of the *Good*.

Given: a series of events, each and all consistent with a specific theorem-lattice. These events are located in time and place. The relevant theorems are determined by an underlying hypothesis. In what part of that span of time and place, does that hypothesis exist? The hypothesis never changes during any part of that span of space-time; it exists, "simultaneously," in all the places and times defined by that theorem-lattice, but is confined to none of them. Meanwhile, that hypothesis is the *necessary and sufficient cause* for the selection of all of the theorems adopted as propositions for the occurrence of the events. In this respect, as *sufficient and necessary cause*, the hypothesis has the form of the *Good*. Yet it is not, otherwise, The Good indicated by Plato, since the existence of the highest Good (*The Good, or Absolute Good*) can not be conditional, can not be the predicate of an hypothesis. Yet, as efficient *necessary and sufficient cause* the Good (*Absolute*) is located in no place or time, but simultaneously in all, just as the hypothesis relevant to a specific theorem-lattice.

Thus, rather than the "Dr. Doolittle 'Pushme-pullme,'" fairy-tale myth of mechanistic causality, commonly taught in schools today, we must have the sense of efficient relationship among past, present, and future, as implicit in the Platonic notions of *hypothesis* and *Good*. If one says, from this latter standpoint, that the future acts to shape the present, or that the present shapes the past and future, it is only in the Platonic sense of hypothesis and Good, that such an efficient role of time is to be premised. It is through the relatively timeless hypothesis which shapes past, present, and future, that these three aspects of a continuing process behave as if they might be efficiently interactive at all times. They do not interact directly, of course! Like the past, the future is presently implicit in the relevant hypothesis (hypothesis, higher hypothesis, or hypothesizing the higher hypothesis), and always implicit in the Good.[41] It is through the mediation of *sufficient and necessary reason* (hypothesis), that the effect, which acts as if from future upon past, occurs.

Rather than speaking of "natural law," let us speak of a "natural-law hypothesis." As an hypothesis, or the Good which we must hope to approximate by the guidance of that hypothesis, the notion of that hypothesis is timeless. It has the functional aspect of Leibniz's notion of *necessary and sufficient reason*.

Thus, in Paul's celebrated *I Corinthians* 13, it is the inclusion of *agapē*, as a controlling axiom within the hypothesis of natural law, which supplies an intimation of Plato's *Good* to the personality of the actor; it is in that *virtù*, rather than the local practical effect of the deed itself, that the Christian source of redemption of the actor's personality is to be found. It is not the commission of the deed which realizes that redemption, but

---

41. One of the pedagogically more accessible illustrations of the principle is found in discussing the implications of conductor Wilhelm Furt-wängler's references to "playing between the notes." For example: Any masterwork composed in the Classical, motivic thorough-composition of Wolfgang Mozart, Beethoven, Schubert, Brahms, et al. (as opposed to the irrelevant, Romantic method of Liszt, Wagner, et al.), is an unfolding of successive cognitively ordered transitions from a single initial set of intervals (e.g., Mozart's K. 475 Fantasy as treatment of J.S. Bach's *A Musical Offering*). The resolution of this process, at the close of the composition, defines the process of development up to that point, as a musical hypothesis. The qualified performer, rather than interpreting the performance of each passage as he, or she comes to it (either arbitrarily, or according to some formal rule), adjusts the interpretation to cohere with the goal to be reached with the final resolution. That "adjustment" in interpretation represents "playing between the notes." So, the master statesman shapes history, and so the wise person shapes the development of his, or her personal life.

Eratosthenes Measures the Earth

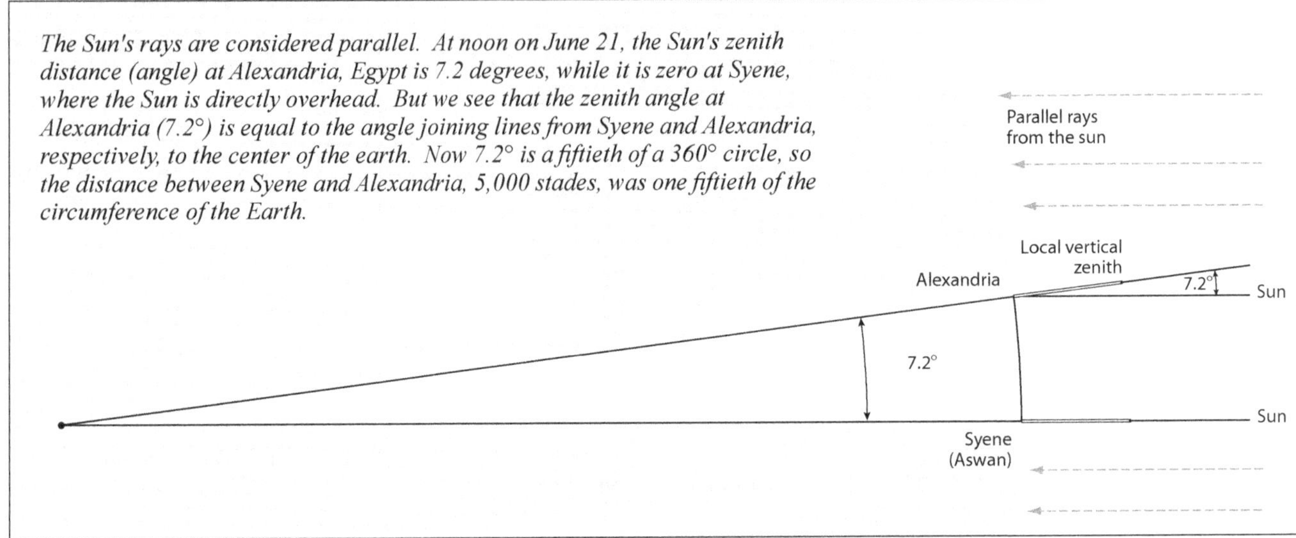

the command of *agapē* not to omit the effective performance of that necessary action. For the Christian, it is the command of agapic reason, to act in imitation of Christ, which contains the virtue, the beauty of the deed.[42]

Nothing occurs without motive. A purely contemplative state of mind does not exist.[43] In human behavior, motive is found in the emotions, of which there are two types. The lower type is the *erotic* impulse, which subsumes the sexual impulse as a special case; it is, more exactly, the passion for objects of sense-perception, actual or imagined. It is the passion of the empiricist, positivist, and existentialist. The higher type, is *agapē*, that which sets the human personality apart from, and above the beasts. *Agapē* references those mental objects which may be strictly classed, inclusively, as *Platonic ideas*: *truth, justice, hypothesis, Good*.

In a competent mode of education, in which text-book learning is rejected, in favor of the student's replicating the original mental act of discovery of valid principles, the student cultivates the experience of *agapē* in those acts of discovery. This is the case in the study of scientific discoveries, and in Classical artistic forms of discovery. It is the joy of this agapic experience, which is the source of the passion for those professions, and the source of the energy of creative-mental concentration, which permits the accomplished scientist, or creative Classical artist, to muster the insight needed for the furtherance of that choice of vocation.

The idea of a principle already known may be recalled by means of a symbolic mode of communication; no *new* idea may be transmitted symbolically, or by deduction. In short, "information theory" is a delusion, a hoax.

Ideas respecting principles, poetic ideas, the central ideas of a Classical tragedy, the musical ideas of great works of Classical musical composition, the ideas of great paintings of Leonardo da Vinci, Raphael Sanzio, or of Rembrandt's "Aristotle Contemplating the Bust of Homer,"[44] and Platonic ideas in general, can not be communicated by means of a literalist, grammatical use of spoken language or deductive mathematics. Such new ideas are communicated, from one person to another,

---

42. One can not suggest that the Creator of the universe is an *impractical* mystic! Those who would be His servants in the administration of this ongoing process of creation, were wise not to overlook the point.

43. Once more, it is appropriate to reference the Schrecker translation. Under "On the Improvement of Metaphysics," Schrecker translates a relevant passage from Leibniz, as follows: "…This force of action, I affirm, is inherent in all substance, and always engenders some action; that is, corporeal substance itself—and the same is true of spiritual substance itself—is never inactive. This does not seem to have been sufficiently understood by those who considered mere extension, or else impenetrability, as the essence of matter, and believed they could conceive a body at rest." p. 83.

---

44. Call that painting what you will. The name which points the viewer directly to the meaning of the painting—its paradox, its *metaphor*!—is "The Bust of Homer Contemplating the Blind Aristotle."

solely by means of *paradoxes*, the which, by their nature must violate a strict grammar of spoken or mathematical language. Another name for such paradoxes, is "metaphor," metaphor as situated amid a nest of ironies.

In various publications, this writer and others have presented the essential features of Eratosthenes' estimate of the length of the Earth's meridian (**Figure 1**). The student who is able to work through replicating the formal mathematical steps of the discovery, may miss the idea involved, unless the teacher makes the point: "How did Eratosthenes give a fair estimate of the size of the Earth's spheroid form, more than 2,000 years before any person saw the Earth's spheroid form?" It is that presentation of that paradox, which impels the student toward discovering, then and there, the meaning of the term "experimental physics." Otherwise, the student might acquire an advanced degree in mathematical physics, without ever discovering the crucial difference between a mere mathematical physics and an experimental physics. Similarly, until the student has confronted himself, or herself with that same paradox (in that or some equivalent form), the student will never recognize the significance of the qualitative difference between astrophysics and microphysics, on the one side, and macrophysics, on the other.

The doctrine, that communication of ideas can be correlated with counting in bits and bytes, belongs in the same receptacle, and institution, to which a sane society relegates Isaac Newton's delusion, that gold might be created out of mud, using such catalysts as a bit of bat's wing and eye of newt.[45] It is through the cognitive solution, by one mind, to paradoxes (metaphors) posed in the utterance crafted by another matter, that the mind of the receiver is able to generate the concept intended by the crafter of the paradox. That conception, so transmitted, leaves no trace of its passage, as a concept, within the literal anatomy of the communication medium employed. The music of Beethoven is not to be found in the score, but in the implications of the paradoxes which the score presents to the adequately developed musician.

The language of science, as the language of Classical forms of poetry, tragedy, music, and painting, is metaphor. The motive of metaphor is *agapē*. The medium of creation, is paradox. The solution of paradox, is accomplished by a reason motivated by *agapē*. That is the meaning of love of truth, and of justice.

How Natural Law Is Applied

The natural law functions as a type of hypothesis, as we have identified "higher hypothesis," above. It consists of a set of principles (e.g., axioms) which govern the forming of many valid hypotheses, each hypothesis subsuming a theorem-lattice of lawful propositions.

Thus, it defines, implicitly, an arguably open-ended set of theorems. These theorems appear in the form of those propositions which have survived the constraints of that hypothesis. Some such theorems are of such a general applicability, either in all societies, or under present forms of society, that we might conveniently attribute them the designation, "constitutional." The way in which the argument for "life, liberty, and the pursuit of happiness" is situated within the 1776 U.S. Declaration of Independence, and the entirety of the *Preamble* in the 1789 U.S. Federal Constitution, are instances of the expression of Leibnizian natural law as constitutional law.[46]

The natural law, in its conveniently compact form, as hypothesis, is composed of a nest, or *manifold*, of discovered principles, in the sense (i.e., experimental physics) we have adduced such principled definitions and axioms, above. A few examples of this are prudently supplied now.

1. *The Ontological Issue.* The record, since Plato, shows, that the worst block to understanding the concept of "natural law," is the same stubborn incompetence respecting what all competent scholars recognize as the crucial *ontological* issue demonstrated by the failure of the character Parmenides, in Plato's famous *Parmenides* dialogue.

To demonstrate that point: *If all elements of a theorem-lattice are efficiently generated by the efficiency of the hypothesis underlying the entirety of that theorem-lattice, is reality located primarily in that hypothesis, or*

---

45. There is no unfairness in this characterization of Isaac Newton. See, John Maynard Keynes on the lunacy which erupted on opening the chest of Isaac Newton's famous chest of laboratory experiments, in "Newton the Man," *Newton Tercentenary Celebration*, (Cambridge, U.K.: Cambridge University Press, 1947).

46. Note, that the Preamble of the Federal Constitution implicitly incorporates those notions of Leibnizian natural law met in the Declaration of Independence, and that the Preamble of the Federal Constitution, within its included "welfare clause," is the fundamental principle of constitutional law of our Federal republic (at least, during those moments of our national history constitutional law has enjoyed better than a sophist's lip-service). On account of that natural-law content of the Preamble, and the Preamble's superior position respecting the remainder of the Constitution, the U.S. Federal Constitution is, by far, the best instrument ever adopted by a nation-state.

in the elements explicitly referenced by a theorem? Or: If one element is the result of a change imposed upon another element, which is more "real," those elements, or the agency which imposes the change upon their existence? Equivalent: *Which is more real, the Creator of the universe, or the elements within that created universe?*

The act of generation of a theorem-lattice is an action of *change*, which is a more efficient existence than any lattice generated by it. The alternate name for that change, is "hypothesis." Special importance must be assigned, therefore, to the agency of *change of hypothesis: higher hypothesis.*[47]

2. *The Definition of Man.* The issue of natural law encountered here, is, specifically, *the definition of man.* This definition must be located from the *origination* of the individual person, as typical of a species which is set, absolutely, apart from the beasts, functionally, by that process which yields this species' not-entropic potential.[48] The definition of man is, thus, to be discov-

ered, by an approach which is focussed upon the source of a society's not-entropic potential.

This distinction of the species, the generation of not-entropic potential, resides in a sovereign quality of the individual person, as individual. The society's, and mankind's not-entropic potential is derived from this characteristic potential of the individual person.

The not-entropic imagery of Riemannian physical geometry, supplies the most readily clear and distinct idea of the relationship between the source of society's not-entropic potential, and the origin of that potential within the sovereign not-entropic potential of the individual person. To wit, the passage of the society from a physical geometry of "n dimensions," to one of "n+1 dimensions."

The increase occurs through a mental act of discovery of what proves to be an original, valid, axiomatic-revolutionary discovery of a principle, within the sovereign mental processes of some person. The transmission of that original "Platonic idea" to other persons, occurs not as "information," but as the use of a representable paradox (metaphor) to trigger a second person, or more, to replicate the mental act of discovery, each within his or her own, sovereign cognitive processes. Only when this discovery is shared, in that metaphorical way, can the discovery be identified by a name assigned to it, among those who have shared the reenactment of the original discovery. The assimilation of that named discovery into the altered practice of the society, is then the means by which the transition from manifold "n," to manifold "n+1," occurs.

Whence manifold "n," that the "n+1th dimension" might be added to it? The original discoverer's first such discovery comes from outside himself, from society. This heritage he acquires through either a process we term "education," or something equivalent in effect.

---

47. This was not only the central issue pitting Plato against the Eleatics, Sophists, and Aristotle; this was the issue of Kepler against the Rosicrucean Robert Fludd and the empiricist Galileo Galilei. It was the issue repeatedly raised in Leibniz's pointing to the source of the incompetence in the method of Descartes, Leibniz's devastating exposure of the hoaxes of Hobbes and Locke, and Leibniz's attack on the incompetence of Newton's method, in the Leibniz-Clarke-Newton correspondence. This fundamental difference in method, underlies the uncompromisable difference of principle which separated the leading American patriots of 1714-1901 from both the British monarchy and the Yankee and pro-slavery varieties of American Tories. For our purposes at this instant, it is sufficient to focus upon the ontological issues implied by "higher hypothesis;" the point has the same immediate implications when applied to the matter of higher hypothesizing and the Good.

48. From the standpoint of experimental physics, this functional definition of man, is mappable in the following terms of analysis situs. The total domain of experimental inquiry is mapped in terms of three qualities of evidence, pertaining to three general types of phenomena. Objects and relations are defined in terms of the scales of (in order of discovery by man) a) macrophysics, b) astrophysics, and c) microphysics. The types of processes considered are (in order of lower to higher ranking) 1) The presumably non-living (organic, inorganic), 2) The presumably non-cognitive living processes, and 3) Cognitive processes. The measurement of scale is in frequency, for which non-linear forms are regarded as higher. The universe of experimental inquiry is shown to be functionally integrated, despite the immediacy of the manifest functional differences of scales and types.

Within the table so ordered, the record of living processes generally, and of man's increase of potential relative population-density through the action of cognitive processes, indicates the general law of the universe: that, from the pinnacle of knowledge of the efficiency of human cognition, the universe as a whole is characteristically a not-entropic process, and that the correlated direction of development of that universe as a whole, as such a not-entropic process, is for the increase of the ration of the universe composed of living and cognitive processes, relative to the so-called "inorganic." In this location, it is sufficient to iden-

tify the fact, that the development of the fictitious, so-called "three laws of thermodynamics" is a myth, concocted by such Nineteenth-century "Fausts" as Lord Kelvin, Clausius, Grassmann, Helmholtz, Maxwell, Rayleigh, et al. The principal arguments advanced on behalf of that concocted myth, derived from the influence of the Malthusian fad of Luigi Botero, Giammaria Ortes, Thomas Malthus, et al., superimposed upon the traditional, arbitrary presumptions inherited from Seventeenth-century empiricism. The Nineteenth-century radical-positivist view, saw all forms of existence as derived from processes primarily rooted in the kinematic imageries of the most radically reductionist interpretation of the inorganic. To carry these wild presumptions into the microphysical realm, there was an axiomatic reliance upon Grassmann's myth, linearization in the very small. Unless we overlook the mythical presumptions underlying the formulation of the so-called "three laws," we can not believe that such "laws" were ever proven.

This inbound transmission occurs in the same mode the original discoverer generates the replication of his mental act of discovery in others; the discoverer acquires the knowledge of the principles in "manifold n," by reenacting the "n" mental acts of original discovery within his own, sovereign cognitive processes.

That simplified description of the characteristic feature of the relevant processes suffices here. It is through the reciprocal process of the cultivation of the individual by the society, and the enrichment of the society's knowledge of principle, by the individual, that not-entropic performance of the society is accomplished.

The larger the ration of the individual members of society who are both educated in this way, and who are afforded the opportunity to express such progress in their daily activity, the greater the rate of progress of the society, relative to any level of knowledge available to any significant part of that society's population.

The same evidence obliges us to recognize, that the society which satisfies the requirement for progress, is characterized by a relatively greater emphasis upon the *agapic*, relative to the *erotic*: that *agapē* must be fostered, or else the creative activity indispensable to progress, will either occur only in diminished degree, or not at all.

The constitutional law of any state must commit that state to serve those principles of progress which we have just summarized. This must be, otherwise, the set of axiomatic moral values which informs the behavior of educators, law-makers, prosecutors, and judges, in particular. Without awarding efficient constitutional authority to those values, life can not be reasonably secure, and freedom, as Leibniz correctly defined it, is not possible.

This brings us to our closing theme: What about "happiness"? The present writer has addressed this in the course of a number of addresses to audiences, during the course of the Democratic Party's 1996 Presidential-nomination campaign. On those occasions, he has referenced this to the *New Testament* parable of the "talents." That argument, and its relevant implication here, are summarized as follows.

When each of us is born, we are given life and a heritage of knowledge, which we may assimilate by reenacting the valid discoveries of principle contributed by preceding generations. That is the talent which is given to us. When we die, if we have returned that talent, enriched by us, to our posterity, and, if we have lived necessary lives in our deeds from day to day, we know that our lives have been necessary for our society, and we may therefore face death with a sense of triumph.

Examine our relationship to society in terms of the knowledge of principles we have received, and those we have transmitted to those who outlive us. Consider, first, our debt to the past.

In the course of reenacting discoveries of principle, it was most pleasing to know the name of the original discoverer, when, where, and how, he or she lived, some general biographical facts, and perhaps acquire an image of that person's face. In reenacting an original discovery, in that moment our mental processes are replicating the internal thought-processes of a person who lived as much as thousands of years ago. One senses one knows that person, from a faraway place, from long ago, better than, perhaps, many "Baby Boomer" husbands and wives come to know one another, these days. Whenever possible, we apply a name of an original discoverer to each of the discoveries attributable to him. It is important that we do so, whenever possible.

When grandparents think of their grandchildren, they are looking toward the future, as if they were putting themselves in the place of, perhaps, one of the important discoverers they had known during their educational years. In terms of both valid discoveries, and good deeds in the spirit of valid discoveries, the good aspects of the past and future of all humanity are made very personal to each of us in our here and now. This is clearest in the instance of those discoveries of principle which bear upon the principle of hypothesis. Hypothesis, as it yearns toward the Good, has its peculiar quality of timelessness. In the Good, all who have lived come together in timelessness; in hypothesis, we have that "intimation of immortality" toward which poor poet Wordsworth might yearn. In that sense of timelessness, the pervasive mood is that of the *agapē* without which cognition were not possible. That sensed moment of timelessness, so achieved, is Leibniz's *happiness*.

As this writer said, repeatedly, during the primary campaigns, "Every person must be assured the opportunity to live in such a manner, that they might die with a smile on their face."

This, the notion of "life, liberty, and the pursuit of happiness," and the common commitment to secure the "general welfare," are those expressions of natural law which ought to be recognized by any competent and decent law-maker, and by every citizen, as that fundamental law of our Federal republic before which all ordinary law must humbly bend. Take such advice from the church, if you will; but take it from a nature whose gospel will be heard, were no sacred book ever written.

9 781977 909923